A Doctor's Guide
To Better Health
Through Palmistry

EUGENE SCHEIMANN, M.D.

A Doctor's Guide
To Better Health
Through Palmistry

Parker Publishing Company, Inc.
West Nyack, N.Y.

PRINTED IN THE UNITED STATES OF AMERICA
13-216861-8 B & P

To June

for her tolerance and love

Acknowledgements

Palmistry carries with it a stigma placed upon it by fortune-tellers and the pseudo-sciences of the Middle Ages. For 25 years I have waged a battle against skeptics to prove what I know to be a fact—palmistry is one of the most reliable methods for determining the genetic and the endocrinologic makeup of an individual. It is an easy, inexpensive method by which the physician can help his patient to a healthy, happy, and full life. My battle with the skeptics has been difficult, and many times my colleagues scoffed at my ideas, although I had adequate data to prove my theories. The editors of *The Journal of Nervous and Mental Disease* were the first to give me encouragement when they published an article of mine in 1948. In 1951 the editors of *The Psychoanalytic Review* renewed my desire to continue my work in medical palmistry by publishing an article of mine. Many colleagues—among them leading psychiatrists of the 40's—inspired me to continue my research by the letters of encouragement they wrote after reading these articles. A letter I received from Dr. Felix Martín Ibáñez, medical director of E. R. Squibb and Sons in 1948, but now Editor-in-Chief of *MD* magazine, gave me special inspiration.

Joseph F. Goodavage, a well-known writer and researcher, is directly responsible for my writing this book. And, I am indebted to him for his encouragement and faith in my work.

The thousands of persons throughout the years who permitted me to examine their hands must remain nameless, but my work could not have been done without their assistance.

My six-year-old grandson, Marc Dimond, is my greatest booster and tells everybody "My grandpa is a famous doctor who can read your palm."

The girls from the library of the American Medical Association gave me much assistance in gathering research materials.

My wife, June, was invaluable in helping to prepare the manuscript. Betty Raffnell assisted with the editing and writing. A special thanks goes to Agnes E. Dillon, who did the final editing and revising of this book. In the beginning she was as skeptical as many of my colleagues, but she soon saw the value of my work and enthusiastically assisted me.

E. S.

What This Book
Can Do for You

Despite the many technical advances in modern medicine, our highly complex laboratory tests, and our diverse diagnostic tools, the personal examination by a physician—based on his hearing, seeing, touching, and smelling—still plays a dominant role in the study and treatment of the sick.

Many times the eye may yield more information than any of the diagnostic mechanical and electronic devices in use today. Before the era of scientific and computerized medicine, our medical ancestors diagnosed diseases by intuition and keen observation. They observed and studied not only the afflicted part, but also the body as a whole. They observed the patient's movements, and they looked at his eyes, his tongue, and, above all, *at his hands*. Palmistry was to them what the stethoscope and the microscope are to the modern doctor. From the hand of their patient, these physicians pieced together information about the personality and temperament of the suffering person and diagnosed ailments more accurately.

Plato, Anaxagoras, and Galen emphasized in their writings the importance of the hand in the study of human beings. Hippocrates, the Father of Medicine; Aristotle, Founder of Psychology; Paracelsus, the Father of Therapeutics; and Dr. Charles Bell, Father of Modern Neurology, all studied the human hand as a diagnostic aid.

With the development of modern scientific methods of diagnosis, however, the use of palmistry in medicine was neglected and in certain respects it was completely discarded. Today we are witnessing a revival of palmistry. It is increasingly recognized as a valuable aid in medical practice. Leading institutions, outstanding doctors, and medical journals of respected stature are recognizing the role of the hand in diagnosis.

I have examined thousands of hands, and I am convinced that the study of the hand could help not only the doctor, but also you, the layman. As you will find out in this book, palmistry can aid you in attaining better health. It will serve as a guide—or a signal—to physical and mental ailments. Through the study of palmistry, you may be able to recognize a *predisposition* to certain diseases, or the possibly unkown *presence* of certain diseases. Palmistry can also help you recognize emotional and mental disturbances before they become evident through other means.

However, I must caution my readers that they must use considered judgment in studying the hand. *None of the lines in the hand is absolute in itself.* To study the whole person it is necessary to study the palm print and handwriting as well as the markings in the hand. The finding of one "bad" sign does not mean that the person has the disease or trait that sign *could* indicate. The study of the hand as a guide to personality and health is a consideration of all the lines of the hand. Also, many "bad" signs are inherited and mean only that your forebears had these markings in their hands.

This book is a guide to better health through palmistry. It is just that—a basic guide. The aim of this book is twofold: (1) to acquaint you, the reader, with the diagnostic significance of the human hand in all aspects of health—physical and also mental; (2) to inspire you to acquire sufficient skill to further develop this presently neglected, yet most significant guide to the art of attaining better health.

EUGENE SCHEIMANN, M.D.

Contents

PART II—HAND PSYCHOLOGY

PART III—THE HANDS—A RECORD OF PSYCHE

I

MEDICAL PALMISTRY

The Principal Lines and Mounts

on Your Palm

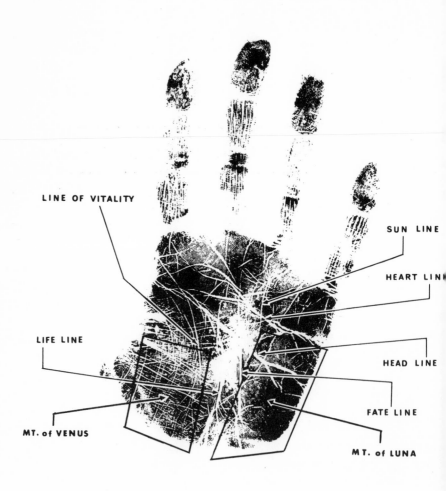

LINE OF VITALITY

SUN LINE

HEART LINE

LIFE LINE

HEAD LINE

FATE LINE

MT. of VENUS

MT. of LUNA

1

The Hand as a Living Computer

Modern scientific medicine is advancing rapidly. New tests and new drugs are being developed at such a fast rate that doctors cannot keep up with them. A doctor can master the new drugs—he only has to ask for literature or samples and try them on his patients, or he can keep on using his old medicine if it is satisfactory. However, he faces a difficult task with the new tests.

As soon as he learns to interpret one test, others come along. He cannot ignore the new tests because, if something goes wrong with a patient or he fails to make a correct diagnosis, he will be severely criticized for not keeping up with the advancement of medicine.

In an effort to relieve this difficulty, the modern doctor, like everyone else today, has been introduced to the *computer*. An estimated 100 medical centers in the United States have been computerized, and many more are projected for the future.

Since medical computers are still in the infancy stage, we cannot at this time make a critical judgment of their value. However, there are many doctors who believe that *computers may*

3

help the doctors but not the patients. It will never be possible to program a computer for empathy, individual experience, and human wisdom—all required to understand the patient as a whole.

Nor will the computer be able to detect the etiological (cause or origin) factors related to temperament, constitution, the unconscious, and certain other nonscientific, nontechnical factors, including such irrational factors as love, libido, and loneliness.

The Use of the Hand as a Computer

There is, however, one computer which has always been with us. It is always available, always accessible, and does not involve complicated laboratory equipment. It can enable the doctor to gain a better insight into the patient's disease, as well as helping him develop a better understanding of the patient as a whole.

This Computer Is the *HAND*

In reference to the significance of this living computer, an editorial in the *Journal of the American Medical Association*[1] has the following to say:

> "Despite widespread and sometimes unnecessary use of numerous laboratory tests in the day-by-day clinical practice, diagnostic methods that require no special apparatus and that depend only on simple observation can play an effective role in obtaining clinical information about patients. In this connection, the human hand is a unique organ from which an extraordinary amount of clinical information may be derived."

Keep in mind that this editorial does not come from a pulp magazine catering to the sensation-seeking mystics. It is from a magazine whose reputation in the medical world is beyond question. Of paramount importance is this editorial's recognition of the study of the hand in the diagnosis of one disease (subacute bacterial endocarditis), "Diagnosis of this disease is sometimes established initially by *information supplied solely by the hand.*" [Italics by author.]

---

[1] Editorial, "The Hand and the Cardiovascular Disease," *JAMA*, February 6, 1954, p. 508.

The editorial concludes with a comment on the hand's role in diagnosing shock, the greatest medical emergency, "The color and temperature of the skin of the hands sometimes yields more information of *impending* shock than either the pulse or the blood pressure." [Italics by author.]

Surely these observations should increase our respect for palmistry as a diagnostic aid rather than cast doubt on the credibility of the *Journal of the American Medical Association.*

The Early Warning System in the Hand

To illustrate the diagnostic significance of the hand, let us consider a common disease such as *arthritis*. We all know that a cure is not yet available for this disease. However, according to the consensus of all arthritis specialists, treatment could generally be satisfactory *if it is started within six months after the first sign of the disease.* One of the reasons for frequent failure of treatment is that the crippling or dangerous so-called rheumatoid arthritis *is not recognized early enough.* This type of arthritis characteristically involves swelling of the knuckles or the joints at the base of the fingers—nearest to the hand. Contrastingly, osteoarthritis, or the mild form of the disease, involves the joints nearest the tops of the fingers. Noting these signs sufficiently early could encourage more effective treatment.

Dr. Theodore J. Berry in his book, *The Hand as a Mirror of Systemic Diseases,* associates certain configurations of the hand with no fewer than 50 diseases! And, the modern medical palmist has linked an abnormal palm print with 19 congenital diseases. Surely, with this weight of testimony in favor of the hand as a diagnostic aid, one would expect medical palmistry to be more widely employed than it is.

Unlike any laboratory test, the hand can give clinical information about diseases and divulge important data about the patient —data closely related to his disease such as his constitutional or endocrinological makeup and his personality.

Glandular Disorders

Every endocrinologist (gland specialist) knows that the hands can reveal the endocrine condition of a person. They know for example that if there is an overactive thyroid, the patient's hand is commonly warm, moist, and trembling, whereas in hypothyroidism (underactive thyroid) it is usually cold, dry, and rough. Dr. Felix Martín Ibáñez, noted writer and onetime professor of the New York Medical College, expressed the significance of the hand in relation to hormones by stating, "The *hand can indeed enable us to cast the endocrinal horoscope* of a patient." [Italics by author.]

Medical Study of Personality Through Palmistry

Palmistry is especially valuable in the study of personality. The hands are open for inspection and do not require the patient's cooperation. This eliminates the probability of *deceptive* conclusion because of the inhibitory mechanism in the subject to misstate significant answers asked of him.

Also the characteristic features of the hand are often evidenced in early childhood when handwriting, Rorschach ink test, and other psychometric or technical tests cannot be applied.

Benefits of This Book for the Layman

All these factors should convince you that the human hand could help doctors practice medicine. But, *what can the study of the hand do for you,* the layman? Consider the following points:

(1) Perhaps the most important benefit you gain is to develop your intuition. This could be invaluable in helping to prevent ailments and aiding the sick through a uniquely intuitive process.

(2) You can help prevent diseases by being more "health conscious" in your daily living. If, like most people, you have an interest or at least a dependency on cars, you become "car-conscious." You may study the car manual or watch the mechanic as he treats your car's ills. You gradually become so familiar with your car that you get to recognize certain noises or certain motor irregularities which indicate that something may be wrong. Similarly, your study of the human hand will give you a familiarity

with this organ which could help you recognize certain irregularities of your body's mechanics. If you love your car, you will take it to a mechanic for a checkup. By being uniquely health-conscious and alert to certain signs, you may consult a physician or urge a friend to seek professional help before a disorder progresses beyond the treatable stage.

(3) In certain cases, especially in psychosomatic ailments (those caused by mental means), you may be able to help someone when medicine fails to do so by giving him faith and hope. This may sufficiently relieve his anxiety and allow nature to effect the cure. Remember, *your palm not only contains warning signals but also offers hope—one of the best medicines for the sick.*

(4) You can persuade others to observe the warning signals they receive from physicians. The modern doctor knows a great deal about the causes of diseases (smoking, too much cholesterol, lack of exercise, drinking, and so on) and offers his patient a healthier way of life; but unfortunately, few patients listen to him. If you could master the study of medical palmistry, you might help persuade many people to live a healthier life.

(5) You can learn a great deal about human nature because the hand gives information to the layman as well as to doctors.

Dr. W.C. Cutler, well-known surgeon for the hand, who spent a lifetime repairing our living computer, says[1] that if one examines it closely, the hand reveals much concerning its owner. In it is written a record of age and sex, health or disease, occupation and habit, skill or inaptitude, accident and misuse, work or indolence. One does not need to know palmistry to read that there is something of the past, a good deal of the present, and even a little of the future in the hand.

---

[1] *The Hand—Its Disabilities and Diseases.* W. B. Saunders Co., Philadelphia, Penn., 1942.

2

How to Study and
Analyze the
Human Hand

P almistry, sometimes called chirology, consists
of two branches: *chirognomy* (character analysis); and, *chiromancy* (fortunetelling). This book will deal purely with a new
form—*scientific* palmistry—a total *hand analysis* of not only disease but also a complete study of the person. It will include chirognomy, but it will completely omit the art of prediction of the
future, despite the fact that in the beginning chiromancy was
the most important part in the treatment of the sick (division
of the hand—*cheri*, hand; *manteia*, divination).

An Ancient Explanation for Sickness

Our medical ancestors and those who practiced healing believed that a man became sick because he committed a sin or

9

offended an evil spirit. The cure of his ailment was the appease-
ment of the god or the evil spirit. The task of the healer was to
diagnose from certain omens the seriousness of the sickness and
the sin of the patient. The most common forms of divination were
palmistry and astrology. To practice this type of "medicine" the
most important requirement was clairvoyance and the power of
suggestion on the part of the "healer." Despite the erroneous and
irrational practices of the healers, the patients seldom lost faith
in them because, if they failed to cure them, the patients were
blamed for their failure to appease the gods!

The modern fortuneteller remains popular because the majority
of his clients always remember his few true predictions, and
conveniently forget all the false ones.

Basics of Medical Palmistry

To become adept at practice of modern medical palmistry, you
must have more than intuition or power of suggestion; you must
have knowledge, reason, and wisdom. If you have these qualities,
you can help your fellowman, as well as yourself, to maintain
better health.

To achieve these beneficial aims you must be guided by the
following rules:

(1) *Be skeptical.* Don't believe this book until you subject it
to analysis, tests, and actual readings. Only in this way will you
learn the most important assets of palmistry. For example, let
us say that a long index finger is a sign of dominance, pride, or a
strong ego (index finger longer than third finger).

Before you accept this statement, observe at least ten people
with long index fingers. If the majority (or at least 80 per cent)
admits to being proud or caring to dominate, then you have a
right to accept this sign. But to be convinced, you should examine
ten people with short index fingers, which signify dependency,
lack of pride, and weak ego. Now, if you again observe eight out
of ten subjects correctly, you can be positive. But suppose you
discover, as is often the case, that many people with the short
finger show dominance, pride, or a strong ego. You must then
learn whether these traits are an overcompensation; you must

find out by questioning his background whether this person is perhaps overcompensating for a weakness. This example emphasizes a very important point—that *the hand shows only tendencies that man can overcome.*

(2) *Beware of fortunetelling.* The purpose of this book is to promote *better health.* Fortunetelling can be very dangerous to anyone who is searching for improvement of physical or emotional health. When you visit someone in the hospital and note that he looks very sick or wan—as if ready to die—don't tell him he looks bad. It may be true, but don't push him into the grave before his time. Likewise, you can be utterly wrong in palmistry if you tell someone that his short or broken life line indicates sickness or early demise. *It is not up to you to predict.* The Oracle of Delphi in ancient times kept her predictions purposely ambiguous, and the modern doctor generally has a hard time making a prognosis. Many times he may predict a patient's death and the patient will ultimately outlive the doctor. On the other hand, he may undertake a complete medical checkup which shows that the patient is in excellent health, and the next day the patient may die. If you are interested in fortunetelling, do it for fun . . . don't take yourself seriously.

(3) *Be humble.* Even if you think you have mastered the art of palmistry, do not be "all-fired" sure. Do not try to impress others with your specialized hand knowledge, but try to learn. A thousand years ago medicine was sure of everything. Now, after millions of case histories, libraries, and clinics, medicine is more mature and more aware of what we do not know. For example, two years ago there was an article in the *Journal of the American Medical Association* which stated that we are not sure about the causes and cure of such a common disease as uncomplicated peptic ulcer.

If the doctors are not sure, you have no right to give a positive diagnosis. You can only tell the subject that the hand indicates certain factors. To find out whether your impression is valid, try to obtain a case history like a physician does; or, let the subject do the talking. Evangeline Adams, the famous astrologer, stated that she learned much more from what people told her than from their horoscope!

(4) *Have confidence in yourself.* Although you should be humble and skeptical, if there is an idea you are convinced of do not be afraid to explore it. Medical palmistry is still comparatively young and can perhaps benefit from new discoveries which will surely come when a wave of laymen enter the field. With sufficient interest, observation, and intuition, you can challenge the experts.

(5) *Do not attempt to practice medicine!* It is illegal, as well as unwise. But, if you want to explore the field of medical palmistry, you should observe the most important procedure in medical practice—*do not predict doom.* Few doctors tell their patients that their condition is hopeless. Unfortunately, many palmists do predict gloomy events. For example some will say, "Your heart line is broken; therefore, you may have a heart attack." Or, they may say that if your life line is short or broken, your life is in danger.

If you are convinced that certain signs indicate sickness, consider the same as a warning signal on the highway—"danger ahead"—"slow down"—"drive with care." You may tell your subject to slow down or take it easy; or, you may warn him to see his doctor.

(6) *Do not depend on one sign alone.* You must study the hand as a whole. You must remember that some diseases or characteristics show up in different ways in different hands. To learn the significance of the total hand in modern medicine, we shall evaluate the following features in the following pages of this book:

    a. hand gestures, postures, and movement;

    b. texture, temperature, and color of the skin;

    c. consistency, flexibility, and moisture of the hand;

    d. the nail;

    e. alternation and abnormalities of the fingers and the palm;

    f. dermatoglyphics—the pattern formed by the dermal ridges on the palms and fingers;

    g. chiroglyphics—the lines and other markings of the palm.

3

How to Understand Gestures, Postures, and Movements of the Hand

A man's first act of communication or expression is the gesture of his hand. As an infant he uses his hand in the formation of image, thought, and expression. It enables him as Dr. Ferenczi,[1] Freud's close collaborator, put it, ". . . not only to signalize such wishes as immediately concern his body but also to express wishes that relate to the changing of the outer world." An infant's first hand gesture is the grasping reflex, which is an expression of his anxiety.

---

[1] *Stages in the Development of the Sense of Reality (Sex in Psychoanalysis)*. Boston: R. G. Badger, publisher, 1916.

Significance of Basic Reflexes

The grasping reflex is so strong in an infant that, if you put the hands of a newborn on a small rod he will hold himself there until released—even if you do not hold him. The newborn baby still represents our ancestors who were tiny, defenseless animals to whom the tree offered sufficient food supply to satisfy their small demands. For them, tree life offered a means of escape from the dangers on the ground. Birth brings a new outer world, which means the beginning of danger and insecurity to the infant. It is still a defenseless animal who grasps the imaginary tree branch firmly or clings to his mother's fur.

The grasping reflex of the newborn demands the return of a state of security he once enjoyed inside his mother's womb. When the infant becomes more acquainted with his frightening new world and becomes more sure of his environment, he will give up his grasping reflex. Dr. H. M. Halverson[2] observed that a newborn who is comfortable quite often fails to exhibit any indications of grasping under repeated stimulation of the palm. The infant clutches firmly at the beginning of feeding and he grasps weakly or not at all at the end of feeding. This shows that there is a very definite relationship between satiation and grasping. Although the child loses his grasping reflex after four or five months, he maintains a grasping-like posture by holding his thumb firmly in his clenched hand, especially if he is disturbed or hungry.

The significance of hand gestures and posture has been recognized by every hand analyst. Dr. Charlotte Wolff, the noted medical palmist, stated that subconsciously executed gestures of the hand are a more valuable mirror of personality than the face because, unlike facial expressions, gestures of the hand are beyond our control and, therefore, are impartial.

This is especially true in gambling. Men with poker faces may deceive all their fellow partners, except those who study their

---

[2] "Studies of the Grasping Responses in Patients with Neurosis, Epilepsy, and Migraine." *Arch. of Neur. & Psy.*, 56:631, 1946.

hands. The significance of hand gestures in relation to the so-called poker face was portrayed very revealingly by Stefan Zweig in his book *Twenty-four Hours in the Life of a Woman,* "Man betrays himself in gambling. I know it's a truism . . . but I maintain that it is the hand that is the traitor. Just because the gambler concentrates his attention on controlling his face, he forgets his hands and he who watches them . . . reads everything from them . . . the hands disclose the innermost personality . . ."

Thumb Characteristics

One of the most revealing characteristics of hand gesture is the thumb. *The thumb represents the ego of the person.* For the first two years of an individual's life he has a completely inactive thumb because his ego has not yet begun to develop. Occasionally some children will make gestures that indicate an active thumb before two years. They hold their thumbs far out from the palm and separated from the other fingers. This shows an already developing ego and the beginning of independent mental attitudes.

I remember well an instance of this precocious thumb development. I visited a colleague of mine and marveled that his month-old daughter held her thumb outside her clenched hand while she slept. Her father replied that she almost never hid her thumb. I prophesied that this little girl would grow up to have a strong ego and would be very independent and secure in her own judgment. On her first birthday, I noticed that she now held her thumb far away from her index finger in an unclenched position and I added to my original prophecy that she would eventually dominate her household. Now every time I see my colleague he reminds me of that prophecy and comments that it was all too true. His little girl has indeed grown up to be a very strong young woman who takes life into her own hands!

Just as a grasping reflex in a child over six months old represents emotional insecurity, an adult who holds his thumb in a clenched fist is manifesting a retrogression to childhood or a state of anxiety. Two other postures of the thumb which also indicate anxiety or emotional stress are when an individual hides his thumb with his other hand and when he bends his thumb and holds it close to his outstretched palm.

Conversely, the thumb that stretches far out from the hand, forming a complete right angle with the index finger (Figure 1), demonstrates that the subject is conscious of his ego. The opposite of anxiety is self-assuredness, and the more the thumb is held away from the index finger, the more that individual shows strength and self-confidence. Although this trait is commonly observed in children, who generally keep their thumbs close to their index fingers or close to their hands, adults who habitually hold their thumb in toward the index finger or close to and bent slightly toward the outstretched palm (Figure 2), are showing that their life is dominated more by insecurity and doubt than by confidence. They are introverted, cautious, self-conscious, and secretive; consequently, they are often "bottled up" emotionally.

The person whose thumb is far from the other fingers is liberal and generous. He usually is friendly and likes to help people. However, he does not like to be closely attached to someone, to be obligated, or to be dominated because he likes freedom and independence.

The index finger also shows independency of movement and a demonstrative, persuasive power. It is the most helpful assistant to the thumb. The beckoning index finger expresses an attempt to make the ego attractive to someone else; or, the pointing index finger emphasizes what it is pointing to. The index finger is also used to accentuate statements (the late President Kennedy used this gesture frequently) or as an authoritative, menacing gesture.

If the index finger and the middle finger are widely separated (Figure 3), the subject is independent in thinking and could be influenced only by reason and logic.

Wide space between the little finger and the ring finger (Figure 4), signifies independency of action. These individuals cannot be forced to do something against their will. They can be persuaded only by love and kindness. They prefer to work alone rather than with a partner or a group.

A person who holds all his fingers separately (Figure 5), is a nonconformist and extremely unconventional; he is a good candidate to be a bohemian, beatnik, or hippy. In contrast, if an individual holds all his fingers closely together (Figure 6) he is a

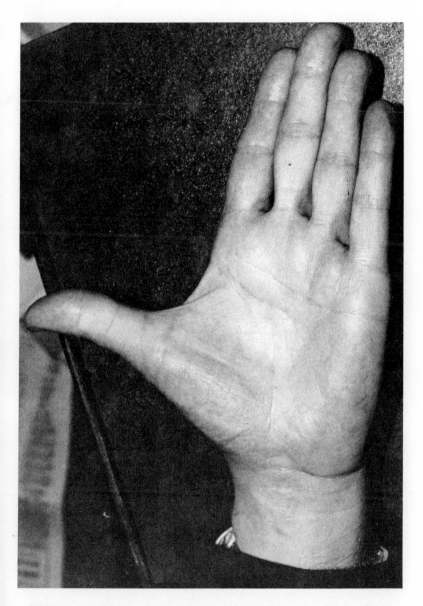

Figure 1. *Widely separated thumb signifies self-confidence.*

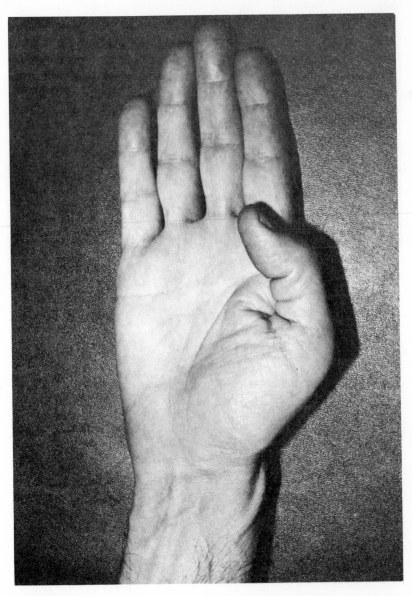

Figure 2. *Closely held thumb denotes lack of self-confidence.*

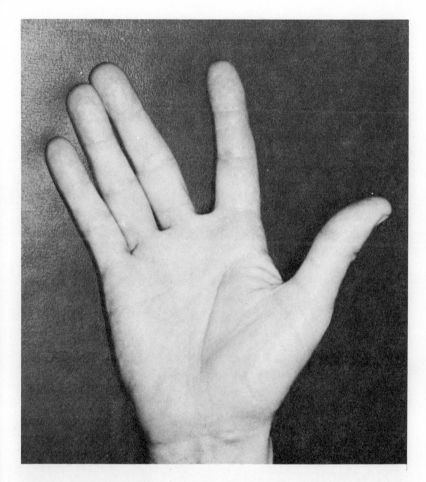

Figure 3. *Widely separated index finger and middle finger is a sign of independent thinking.*

slave of formality or conventionality. He usually is stingy and self-centered.

One of the most expressive gestures is when a person hides his hand from sight as he enters and crosses your office or a room; it is an indication that he has ideas which he does not wish to have exposed. He is probably deceitful or hypocritical. It is also a very significant gesture of schizophrenics.

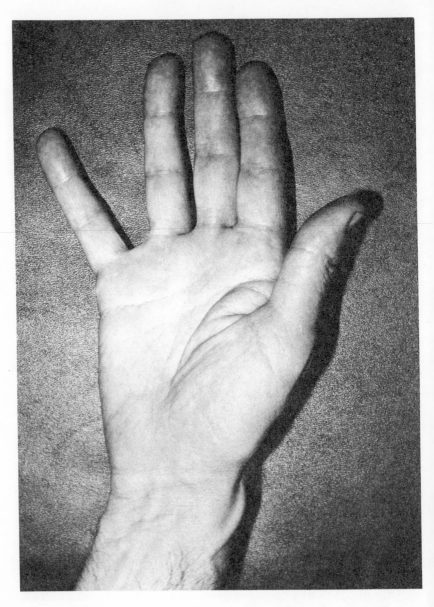

Figure 4. *Wide space between little and ring fingers is an indication of independence of action.*

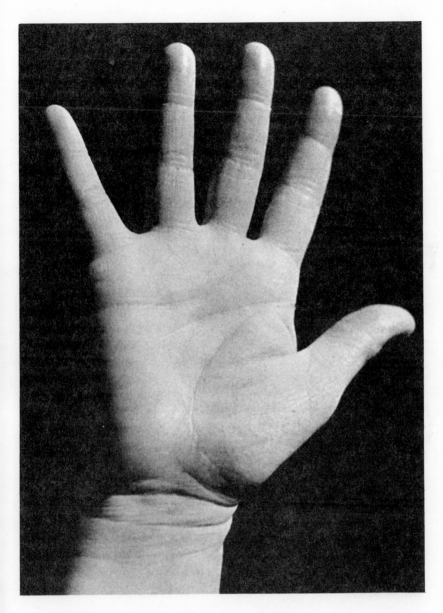

Figure 5. *Widely spread fingers in hand of a nonconformist.*

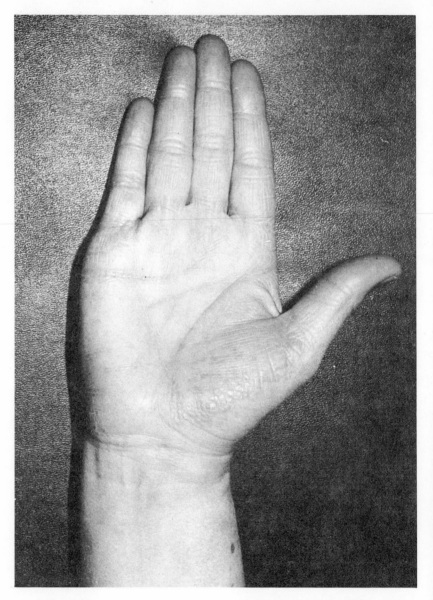

Figure 6. *Closely held fingers is a sign of a conformist.*

Hand Movements Analysis

Walter Sorell, in his book *The Study of the Human Hand,*[3] stated that movements of the hand are instinctive and we become aware of them only if they are used excessively or if our attention is called to them. My observations agree with Sorell's that the position of the hands, the movements of the hands, and gestures with the hand tell much about a person.

Persons whose hands are separated in repose are self-assured, calm, and spontaneous. Persons who keep their hands together are never as free or able to follow impulses as those whose hands are separated.

The principal movements of the hands are in vertical and horizontal directions, and I will discuss some of the more common ones. The offering gesture—a horizontal movement with palms open and turned upward—shows a hand that conceals nothing and a willingness to cooperate. However, people who use this gesture often make poor diplomats because they are too outspoken. Hands which move forward in a partly horizontal direction are seen in realistic people, especially if the fingers are short and fat. However, this movement is seldom seen in even-tempered, balanced people. When the hands move in a vertical direction with the palms outward and the hands close to the body at chest level, the individual is retreating behind a "wall," e.g., the person is prepared for attack and is preparing to resist. When the arms are outstretched with this gesture, the person is not only prepared for an attack but is also ready to carry on the fight.

The chopping gesture is seen in highly emotional and resolute people with a tendency toward being an extrovert. Crossed arms held to the chest, which appear to be a gesture of relaxation, indicate defense and defiance. This movement is seen, for instance, in a child who does not dare to verbally contradict an adult. The desire to hide one's hands in a pocket, behind the back, behind a table, etc.—indicates anxiety which forces the person to protect his ego by hiding it. The event causing the anxiety may have

[3] The Bobbs - Merrill Co., Indianapolis, Ind., 1967.

happened long ago, but the gesture is a subconscious expression of the remaining trauma.

Although I have given only a few examples of involuntary, instinctive gestures of the hand, the gestures and movements are as varied and unlimited as man himself.

One of the most informative, expressive movements of the hand is handwriting. If we are interested in the study of the human hand, we cannot ignore handwriting because it is related to muscular contraction or tension and to the expressive movement of the hand. I must emphasize that personality cannot be judged accurately by any single method; however, graphology, (handwriting analysis,) could be an invaluable aid in evaluating some of the findings of the palmist.

As we mentioned previously, the long index finger symbolizes dominance, pride, and a strong ego—in contrast, a short index finger shows a tendency toward dependency, weak ego, and lack of pride. However, there are individuals who never developed this pride or their egos because of some adverse environmental influence. Many others who have a short index finger are able to nullify a tendency to develop an inferiority complex because of strong environmental influences, and become self-confident. These apparently paradoxical findings could be determined by their handwriting—strong ego, vanity, and dominance will be revealed by high and ornamental capitals or heavy writing.

A comparison of the psychodiagnostic findings of palmistry and graphology will be made in a later chapter.

Diagnostic Aids—Finger and Hand Movements

The posture of the fingers and movements of the hand are important diagnostic aids. If, for instance, the thumb tends to remain bent and the palm is not outstretched but the rest of the fingers are bent, you may suspect oncoming or existing spastic paralysis (Figure 7).

In such paralysis, the patient has difficulty in straightening his fingers and thumb. In contrast is the flaccid type of paralysis—not only can he extend his thumb but he can place it in back of the index finger (Figure 8).

Figure 7. *Flexed fingers in spastic paralysis.*

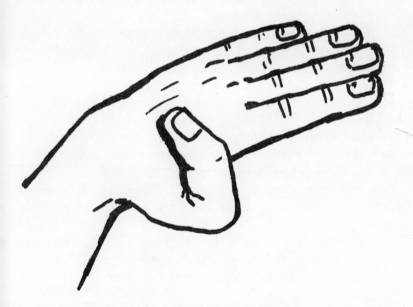

Figure 8. *Extremely flexible thumb in flaccid type of paralysis.*

The *involuntary movement of the hand*—tremor—is a very common symptom of nervous disorder, certain toxic states, and internal disease. The following are the chief varieties of tremor:

Familiar Tremor: It is often congenital and appears in the second and third decade; it usually affects the male sex. It has no relation to any diseases. It is a fine, rhythmic trembling which tends to be increased by emotion, especially if the individual is aware of being watched. He is usually self-conscious because he gives the impression that he is nervous, alcoholic, or a drug addict. Sometimes he is told to have a physical checkup, especially by his employer, because he may have a disease and is not suitable for a certain job.

We may include the senile tremor in this category. It is very similar to the familiar tremor, except it is not increased by emotion or tension; rather, it is aggravated by movement of the hand. It is often associated with shaking of the head and occurs in the fifth or sixth decade.

Parkinson Tremor: It is easily recognized by the so-called "pill-rolling" movement of the index finger and the thumb. The trembling is coarse and of a large amplitude; there usually are between four to eight movements a second.

This tremor is present at rest and it is increased by excitement; occasionally it stops when the patient uses his hand. It is the most characteristic symptom, as the name implies, to Parkinson disease; but, it sometimes occurs if there has been a head injury or carbon monoxide poisoning or if there is arteriosclerosis of the brain.

Cerebellar Tremor: In contrast to Parkinson tremor, cerebellar tremor is fine and rhythmic. It is absent at rest, and becomes evident when the person approaches an object such as touching his nose or lifting a cup to his mouth. Therefore, it is called *intention* tremor. It is an important diagnostic sign of multiple sclerosis.

Toxic Tremor: This type occurs in poisoning or intoxication from various sources such as mercury, copper, alcohol, barbiturates, and narcotics. It disappears when the patient gets rid of the poisoning.

If the tremor is caused by alcohol, it may be a clue to diagnosing an alcoholic. A young man who came to me was worried about the girl he was in love with and wanted to marry because he had been told she was an alcoholic. He had been advised to observe her for a week and if she drank liquor in the morning it would indicate she was an alcoholic. He did this and told me she never asked for a drink in the morning. I then asked him to watch her when she first got up in the morning to see if her hands shook. He said that both her hands and her lips shook. Evidently this girl, who was an alcoholic, had controlled her desire for a drink but she could not control the tremor in her hands. Tremor in this case was an indication of alcoholic addiction.

Liver Tremor: A symptom of liver disturbance, it resembles the Parkinson tremor except it is not associated with rigidity, which is very characteristic of Parkinson disease. It is increased when the patient holds his arms out at his side. It resembles a wing-beating motion. Such a tremor, as Dr. T. Berry pointed out, is an important indicator of early decompensation of liver function.

Thyroid Tremor: A sign of an overactive thyroid gland is fine trembling which is amplified if the individual stretches and spreads his fingers. The hand characteristically is wet and warm and has smooth or satinlike skin.

Nervous Tremor: The most common trembling of the fingers is associated with fear, anxiety, and hysteria. Unlike the others, this tremor has no pattern. It is not rhythmical but coarse and irregular. To differentiate this tremor from another, the subject would be given a tranquilizer and his reaction watched. In most instances the trembling will stop. However, a condition resembling a nervous tremor can be brought on by low blood sugar; sometimes this is a result of dieting. In these instances, instead of a tranquilizer, the person should be given orange juice or sugar. If the trembling stops, the cause is low blood sugar and not nerves.

4

The Meaning of Skin Texture, Temperature, and Color

The famous smile of Leonardo da Vinci's Mona Lisa has captured the imagination and curiosity of many observers. Her smile may be mysterious or even deceitful, but her hands are not mysterious to the experienced observer. The smooth texture of her hands indicates that she has noble characteristics!

If you meet a person with a similar smile, feel her hand, and if you find that the skin is smooth and warm, you can consider her smile genuine.

Texture and Temperature Are Important Signs

The texture and the temperature of the hand has long been an important sign to doctors and palmists from ancient times. Doctors have always considered skin texture and temperature to be a barometer of mood, disposition, age, and health. When people are healthy, happy, and young, the skin is smooth, elastic, and warm. When a person is sick, old, or has a bad disposition, his skin is probably wrinkled, coarse, or cold and clammy.

A fine, soft skin texture which is slightly coarser than a baby's hand signifies a refined and emotionally impressionable person who doesn't like anything that is rough and coarse. He will avoid the company of vulgar people and reluctantly do rough work such as washing dishes and hard labor. On the other hand, a skin which is coarse, hard, or wrinkled indicates a coarse individual who is quarrelsome, critical, rough, and loves manual labor.

Glandular Conditions Indicated

The texture of the skin is determined by our hormones, which also control our personality. Therefore, we could consider *skin texture as an indicator of our inner nature.* As the famous palmist W. Benham put it, "Refined texture softens everything; coarse texture animalizes it."

Because of the close relation between the texture of the skin and the endocrine glands, skin texture and temperature as we mentioned previously, are important diagnostic signs in thyroid disorders. In the case of overactive thyroid glands (hyperthyroidism) the skin is smooth, satinlike, and warm; whereas, in the hand of a person with hypothyroidism (underactive gland) the skin is doughy, dry, cold, and coarse. There are times when the hand is a better diagnostic tool than modern equipment, as the following example illustrates.

A woman who was fatigued, tired, and very nervous went for a physical examination. The doctor gave her a complete checkup, and all the laboratory tests were negative. She was not satisfied with this doctor's findings and came to me. Her hands were doughy, dry, rough, and cold, and her nails were brittle. I immediately suspected that she might have an underactive thyroid gland. When taken previously, a basal metabolism test had been negative. I repeated the test, which was again negative. Because her hands indicated a thyroid deficiency and I could find no other evidence of another disease causing her symptoms, I prescribed thyroid medication. In three months she improved considerably, including the condition of her hands; they were warmer and the nails were firmer.

Alterations in Skin Temperature

The temperature of the skin can give definite information concerning changes in the blood circulation of the hand. In evaluating these changes, you must consider the temperature of the room and the interval between the time the subject was outdoors and the time of the examination of the hand.

In winter, if the hand of a person remains cold despite the warm indoor temperature or if the hand is persistently cold in any kind of temperature, you must think of a circulatory disorder called vasospasm, a constriction of the tiny blood vessels (capillaries) in the hand. The vasospasm is controlled by our nervous system. If the nerves are stimulated, changes will take place. The most common stimulants are drugs (such as adrenalin), certain illnesses, starvation, cold, and emotion.

The nerves will constrict the blood vessels if there is pain, fear, anxiety, and so forth and the hands will become cold and clammy. The blood vessels will be dilated and the hands will be warm if, for instance, the person undergoes a satisfactory sexual experience. I have observed that many patients of mine who suffer from insomnia and sexual frustration have cold, clammy hands.

The best way to determine the skin temperature is to check the back of the hand and the palmar surface of the fingers. It is important that you compare the temperature on both hands. A difference in skin temperature between the two hands is an indication that some local, abnormal condition (such as blockage of the circulation of the colder hand) exists and that the person should be referred to a doctor.

Color of the Hand

The blood circulation not only determines the temperature, but also the color of the hand.

The normal color of the hand is rosy or pink. Any other color is an indication that there is something wrong with the health or with the temperament of the individual. And, it is not an exaggeration to state the color and temperature of the hand is a vital sign of life and death because *the hand is an indicator* of our cardiovascular system.

Types of Color Changes

There are three main color changes in the skin: 1. Rubor, 2. Pallor, and 3. Cyanosis, which are described below:

1. *Rubor, or extreme redness,* is generally associated with the increased temperature of the hand which occurs when the blood vessels are dilated.

One disease in which the blood vessels are dilated is erythromelagia. The chief symptoms of this disease are increased skin temperature and an extreme redness of the palm, which are accompanied by a burning or tingling sensation and profuse perspiration. The disease sometimes occurs suddenly in response to exercise or heat and last minutes or hours. At other times, it is associated with internal diseases such as high blood pressure, gout, rheumatoid arthritis, and diabetes.

In a condition known as palmar erythema (or "liver palms"), rubor is limited to only a part of the hand, usually a part of the hand which would come in contact with a surface (such as in taking a palm print). This condition is common in persons with a liver disease and in pregnant women. It is also associated with various vitamin deficiencies and chronic pulmonary tuberculosis.

2. *Pallor or paleness of the skin* is accompanied by decreased temperature. It is the most important sign of anemia or anxiety. A great service you could do for a person having these signs is to recognize early anemia or some internal bleeding. Extend and bend back the person's palm. If you notice that the main crease lines are pale, the best thing that person can do is to go to his doctor because chances are he has anemia or an internal hemorrhage. Occasionally, a pale or white hand is also a sign of a poor characteristic trait. Persons with pale hands are often unrealistic, selfish, and unemotional. Whereas, a person whose hands are an intensive red usually have an extremist attitude in their behavior and thinking.

3. *Cyanosis or bluish discoloration* of the hand occurs most frequently in congestive heart failure, congenital heart diseases,

and local circulatory disturbances. Unlike the other color changes, cyanosis is accompanied by either increased or decreased temperature. The warm, bluish hand may tell us that there is something wrong with the general blood flow, while a cold, bluish hand may indicate that there is a local circulatory disorder or some degree of persistent vasospasm.

Perhaps the most significant sign in cyanosis is when a warm, pale hand becomes suddenly cold and bluish; this is one sign of an impending shock.

There is one interesting disease where you find all th. ee of the colors—Raynaud's disease—which occurs most often in young women who have an underactive thyroid gland.

Raynaud's disease is a vasospastic disorder precipitated by cold or emotional distress. The tips of the fingers of both hands first become pale, then cyanotic, then an intensive red, with throbbing and swelling. The attack usually ends spontaneously after the patient calms down or after placing the hand in warm water. Advise a subject with this disease to always wear warm gloves and keep a hand warmer in his pocket, because several attacks may cause some painful lesions and possibly gangrenous ulcers.

5

How to Observe Consistency and Mobility of the Hands

According to the Hindus, palmistry has three main functions: Darsana (seeing), Sparsana (touching), and Rekha Vimarsana (reading the lines). In the previous chapter, we emphasized the importance of Darsana (observing the gesture and color of the hand). We also mentioned the diagnostic significance of Sparsana (testing the texture and temperature of the hand). In this chapter, we shall evaluate an equally essential part of touching, the palpation of the muscular tone or vigor of the hand. In other words, we shall interpret the *consistency* of the hand. We shall also analyze the movement or the mobility of fingers, because the movement of the hand is closely related to the consistency of the hand.

Consistency an Indicator of Energy

The consistency of a hand, which is marked by its resistance to pressure, is a sure indication of the quantity of energy possessed by a person. The consistency is determined by the muscular

33

development and the fatty deposits of the hand. Based on these factors we could classify hands into three types: (1) the flabby hand; (2) the firm hand; and (3) the hard hand. These types are discussed below:

1. *The flabby hand* is characterized by a lack of muscular tone and lack of resistance to pressure or palpation. This type of hand is usually small, broad, fat, and flabby. The fingers are very soft and "boneless," resembling a small sausage. This type of hand is often present in persons who have a sluggish or *underdeveloped thyroid gland*. Such people love worldly pleasures, comfort, and luxury. They like to eat, drink, and be merry. Possessors of such a hand have no willpower or self-discipline to control their pleasure-seeking instincts. Although these people are friendly and very sociable, they are generally unreliable.

2. *The firm hand* is firm because it contains more muscle and less fat. Despite its firmness there is some degree of elasticity. In comparison to the flabby hand, where the keynote is lack of energy or laziness, the firm hand is a sign of activity, vigor, and energy. People with a firm hand are usually reliable and have positive personalities. They try to prove their friendship with deeds and action.

3. *The hard hand* is very firm, has a strong resistance to pressure. It is an obstinate, unreceptive hand indicative of a person filled with an immense store of energy which must be expended in physical labor. The hard hand is large and the skin has a coarse texture, signifying that the subjects are less refined and usually less intelligent or cultured. These people have a tendency to acquire complexes which shut them off from others by hardening themselves to the outside world. The hard hand, unlike the flabby hand, has an extreme form of rigidity, which brings us to a very important part of palmistry—the mobility or flexibility of the hand.

The Importance of Mobility of the Hand

The mobility of the hand reflects mobility of the mind and emotion. As Benham put it, "Flexible hands show a flexible mind, and stiff hands a stiff mind." Some hands are so flexible that the finger can be bent back almost at a 45 degree angle, and others are so rigid and cramped that the fingers cannot be straightened.

A rigid or stiff hand is indicative of a contracted or a non-adaptable personality. Such a person is reserved, more or less egotistical, stubborn, and often stingy. A flexible hand denotes adaptability, versatility, and generosity. If flexibility is extreme, there is danger that the individual will have a tendency to diversify his energy or talent, thus becoming a "jack of all trades." Another danger to persons with extremely flexible hands is that they will be easily influenced by others and become slaves or easy victims of undesirable people.

Points to Observe

I have observed that there is a definite relation between the mobility of the hand and the space between the upper and lower transverse (flexion) lines. The space is very narrow in the hand of a person with an extremely contracted personality (see Figure 9), whereas in the hand of a person with a flexible personality the space is wide (Figure 10).

Figure 9. *Palm print of contracted personality.*

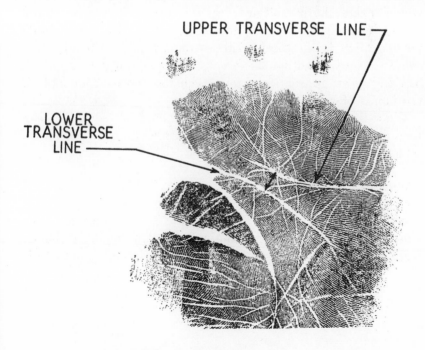

UPPER TRANSVERSE LINE

LOWER TRANSVERSE LINE

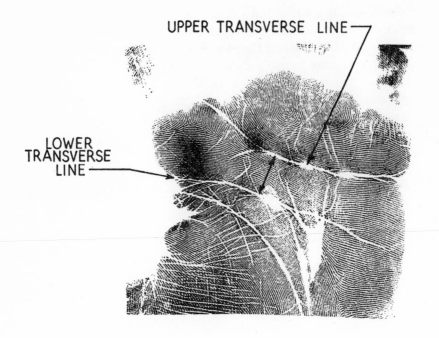

UPPER TRANSVERSE LINE

LOWER TRANSVERSE LINE

Figure 10. *Palm print of released personality.*

In cases of extremely flexible personalities, we often find an additional flexion line at the base of the fingers (Figure 11), which makes the overall spacing very wide. This extra flexion crease results from separate movement of the ring and middle fingers. Such is the case in an extremely mobile hand whose owner is very sensitive to nervous and emotional stimuli. The marking often appears in many psychiatric patients, notably in the hands of schizophrenics.

When the mobility of the hand and spacing between the crease lines are equal in both hands, we can assume that the person will seldom change.

Changes in Mobility

The marking of the palm never changes, but there are times when the *mobility changes* in the dominant hand. If the left hand is flexible and the right is rigid, the individual's personality

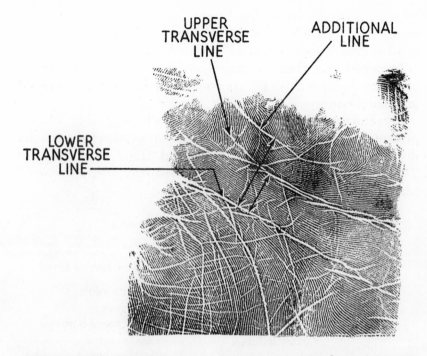

UPPER
TRANSVERSE
LINE

ADDITIONAL
LINE

LOWER
TRANSVERSE
LINE

Figure 11. *Hand print of extremely released personality. Note additional flexion lines. Space between all three lines, as indicated by small arrows, must be considered.*

has become more rigid; he has become more cautious, stingy, and less versatile or adaptable. If the left hand is stiff and the right is flexible, his personality has become more released and flexible.

These changes are more revealing if we study the handwriting of the individual because there is a definite relation between the flexibility of the fingers and the handwriting.

Contraction and Release Connotations

The keynote of modern handwriting analysis is the so-called contraction and release hypothesis. According to the experts, if the person's handwriting is considerably contracted, his personality also is contracted. On the other hand, if his writing is very loose or released, his personality will be flexible. When contraction is predominant, the handwriting will be cramped and restricted; when release is predominant, the writing will be expanded and loosely executed.

I noticed that there is some correlation between contracted or released personality, the consistency or mobility of the hand, and handwriting.

My findings are summarized in the following table which I presented in an article entitled "The Comparison of the Psychodiagnostic Findings of Graphology and Hand Psychology" in *The Journal of Nervous and Mental Disease*, Vol. 107, No. 3, March, 1948.

TABLE I — Table of Comparisons

	Handwriting	*Structure of Hand*
Contracted	Slowness Contraction of letters Narrow, cramped writing Narrow letters Excessive pressure Carefully drawn letters Deliberate regularity	Immobile joints Stiff fingers Narrow space between flexion lines Well-developed muscular pattern Heavy, thick, and short fingers Uniformity of crease line
Released	Speed Amplification of letter contours Wide, loose writing Wide letters Little pressure Simplified letters Irregularity	Mobile joints Flexible fingers Wide space between the flexion lines Lack of muscular development Long, thin fingers Irregularity of crease line pattern

Graphology is also valuable when there is a discrepancy between the mobility of the finger and the thumb. There are instances when the fingers are flexible and the thumb is rigid or firm-jointed. Other times the fingers are stiff and the thumb is extremely flexible or double-jointed.

I believe in such a contrast the finger denotes the attitude of the individual with respect to his material possessions. Handwriting analysis can help you determine the true character of the subject.

If a person has flexible fingers but a rigid thumb, he will give money or presents, but he will not become involved with anyone. If he has a flexible thumb and stiff fingers he will be emotionally extravagant but not materially extravagant. He will do everything for a friend as long as it does not involve any financial or material sacrifice.

6

What the Nails Can Indicate

Some general systemic diseases, such as congenital circulatory disorders, syphilis, endocrine disturbances, the anemias, and other diseases, leave imprints in the fingernails. Therefore, the study of the nails should be an important part of your hand analysis.

The nail "beds" (at the point of coming out of the finger) are usually the simplest and easiest place for determining cyanosis (bluish discoloration), pallor, and pulsation. They are usually the first places where you could observe an early sign of jaundice or gall bladder or liver diseases.

A doctor using a special type microscope (capillaroscope) could detect a very early sign of diabetes, arteriosclerosis, or mental disease. Emotional disorders may change the nails in the form of pitting, thinning, and splitting.

Dr. A. Hauptman,[1] a noted psychiatrist, found 88 per cent of 304 constitutionally neurotic persons showed abnormal capillaries

---

[1] "Capillaries in Finger Nail Fold in Patients with Neurosis, Epilepsy, and Migraine." *Arch. of Neur. & Psy.,* 56:631, 1946.

(tiny blood vessels) in the fingernail, whereas only 4 per cent of the patients with acquired neurosis showed abnormal capillaries. In a later study, he observed that most of the schizophrenic patients had immature capillary formations resembling the capillaries of children and infants. He also found that most of the patients with manic-depressive psychosis had twisted capillaries. It appears that the *immature capillaries* reflect the *immature mind* of the schizophrenic and the twisted capillaries denote the twisted mind of the manic-depressive (extremely mentally depressed) patient.

In certain diseases where the blood circulation is poor, the cuticles will widen and the nail fold will become thin. In some cases of hardening of the arteries, the blood supply to the nails is diminished and the nails become twisted and distorted. Therefore, we could conclude that certain malformations of the nails are diagnostic signs of physical as well as mental health.

Dr. Theodore J. Berry associated 24 nail configurations with different diseases. In this chapter, we shall evaluate only the most common and revealing nail symptoms as follows below.

Hippocratic Nails

One of the classical diagnostic signs known to every medical student is the Hippocratic nails which sometimes are called "watch glass nails." They are frequently found in tuberculosis, lung tumors, chronic heart disease, and in cirrhosis of the liver. The nails, as the name indicates, are lustrous and curved in the shape of a watch crystal (Figure 12).

Figure 12. *Watch glass nails.*

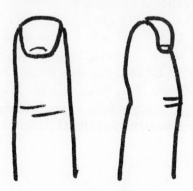

They often accompany the so-called clubbed fingers, which we will discuss in the next chapter. The color of the nail is generally blue (cyanosis). Dr. V. Pardo Castello, a dermatologist who specializes in diseases of the nails, observed that nails and fingers become normal if the patient recovers either from tuberculosis or after surgical correction of a congenital cardiac disorder.

Spoon Nails

The spoon nails, (Figure 13) unlike the watch crystal nails, are concave on the outer surface and are found in nutritional deficiencies, syphilis, skin disorder, hypothyroidism (underactive thyroid gland), and mental defectives.

Figure 13. *Spoon nails.*

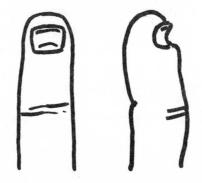

Beau's Lines

This nail abnormality is named after Dr. Beau, who discovered it in the middle of the 19th Century. It consists of horizontal or transverse ridges (Figure 14) which start at the root and move toward the top as the nail grows. Since it takes about 160 days for a nail to grow, it is often possible to determine the date of illness which produced these lines. Beau's lines are associated with acute infection; diseases such as scarlet fever, influenza, and typhus; accidental traumas; nutritional deficiencies, and nervous shock.

Figure 14. *Beau's lines.*

Mee's Lines

Similar to Beau's lines are the so-called Mee's lines. They are transverse white lines but do not cause any ridge or dent in the nails. They occur in high fever, arsenical poisoning, and coronary heart disease.

Longitudinal Ridges

Unlike Beau's lines, these ridges are longitudinal and are of longer duration because they are associated with chronic diseases such as chronic colitis, long-standing skin disorders, and hyperthyroidism (overactive thyroid gland), and they are most important in rheumatic conditions. The longitudinal ridges could be hereditary and they often are an indication of a rheumatic predisposition, especially if there is evidence of this condition in the family. Therefore, if you notice these ridges in a child, it could be well to advise the parents to be alert for early signs of rheumatic fever or rheumatic arthritis, and to see a doctor about the child.

Nail Symptoms in Endocrine Disturbances

As we mentioned previously, the development or growth of all the hand structures are determined by the endocrine glands. Therefore, the alteration of the nail could indicate glandular disturbances. Dr. Charlotte Wolff[1] stated that she had several

---

[1] *The Human Hand*, New York, A. A. Knopf, Inc., 1944.

times diagnosed pituitary and thyroid malfunction from the nails when no clinical symptoms were present. She summarized her findings as follows:

1. The thin, brittle, ridged, short, and "moonless" nail is indicative of an underdeveloped thyroid gland, also a sign of underactive gonads (sex glands) and the pituitary gland. If this type of nail is found in a broad, spongy hand with sausage-shaped fingers and a tapered little finger, it is an indication of hypothyroidism. If the hand is slim and flexible and the little fingers are deformed and shorter than normal, the nails signify underactive gonads. In the hand with broad, square, very flexible, and short fingers, this type of abnormal nail indicates hypopituitary function.

2. The long, narrow, shiny nail with a large moon is a sign of hyperthyroidism.

Nail Symptoms in Nervous and Mental Disorders

In the beginning of this chapter, we emphasized the diagnostic value of the capillaries in reference to nervous and mental disease. There are other equally important signs which you could easily recognize without a microscope or even a magnifying glass. The most common of these signs are the white spots which, according to many physicians and palmists, occur in tired, tense, nervous patients, and disappear when anxiety and stress disappear. If you find these spots, you may assume that the subject is suffering from some situational anxiety or depression.

Another sign of neuroses is the softened, fan-shaped nail (Figure 15). People with this type of nail are very sensitive and are seldom satisfied. They are fault finding and typical naggers.

The long and narrow nail (Figure 16), which occurs more frequently in women, is also an indication of nervousness. The possessors of such nails are usually frustrated artists, actors, and intellectuals who have trouble expressing themselves.

The very short nails (Figure 17) are a sign of a peculiar neurotic behavior which is characterized by an urge to contradict everyone and to argue, even if the person is convinced that he is wrong and the opponent is right.

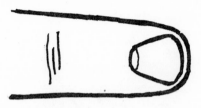

Figure 15. *Fan-shaped nails.*

Figure 16. *Long, narrow nails.*

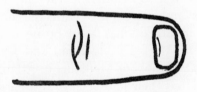

Figure 17. *Short nails.*

According to Dr. Wolff, nail diagnosis is still in its infancy, and much interesting research work is open to physicians and psychiatrists. Perhaps some of my readers will do their own investigations, particularly in the field of psychosomatic diseases (physical illness having a basis in a person's emotions).

7

The Significance of
Alterations of the Fingers
and the Palm

Recently I was elated to read in a national news magazine as well as in other sundry publications, that my own observations and experience with the importance of the hand in relation to disease has been borne out by medical research done by Dr. Mark E. Silverman and Dr. J. Willis Hurst of Emory University School of Medicine in Atlanta. These doctors of medicine presented their latest heart and hand findings to the American College of Cardiology, and the resulting excitement about their conclusions reached past the medical profession to the public domain of a national magazine and wire services. The bulk of their research led them to state that a skilled physician's careful observation of the hands will yield valuable clues *a stethoscope and even an electrocardiograph do not disclose*. In addition, they found that more than 30 different types of heart disease can leave distinguishable marks on the hands. We have already covered much of the known material relating to the hands in general and to the nails, but we will now cover a most important part of medical palmistry in relation to disease—the changes that occur in the fingers and the palm.

The Signs of Heart Disease

Heart disease is often associated with changes in the fingers, such as "clubbing." Clubbing of the fingers is a thickening of the tissue of the fingertip. When the circulation in the heart or lining of the heart is poor, the ends of the fingers often become swollen and bluish. This condition is called clubbing because the fingertips are rounded like a club (Figure 18).

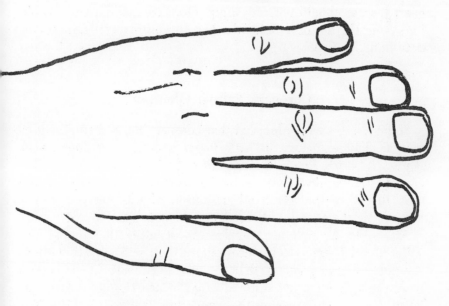

Figure 18. *Clubbing of the fingers.*

Usually clubbing is long standing; but, with heart disease, a *clubbing of previously normal fingers* is the clue to the disorder. However, some healthy, teen-aged boys may show this phenomenon as a normal, inherited, family trait. Dr. Silverman also pointed out, "Warm, moist hands with a fine tremor and occasionally clubbing of the fingers suggests the possibility of an *overactive thyroid* with *resulting inefficiency of the heart* and twitching of its upper chambers. A cold hand with coarse, puffy skin may be due to an underactive thyroid and be associated with fluid in the heart sac, a high blood level of cholesterol, and even necrosis of part of the heart muscle from a coronary occlusion."

Clubbing of the fingers usually is associated, as we mentioned in the previous chapter, with Hippocratic nails and is most common in lung or heart disease. It is considered an important diagnostic sign.

Since clubbing as an indication of certain diseases can be seen in childhood before other symptoms appear, it is wise to examine the hand of any child who tires easily and does not keep up with other children. Children who, for instance, have heart disease should not run, jump, etc. You may be responsible for saving the life of a child who has an *undiscovered disease by examining his hand.*

Coronary Palmar Changes

Some doctors have observed that coronary heart disease causes palmar changes below the little finger and the ring finger, near where the heart line is located. They believe that coronary diseases irritate a nerve center near the heart which is related to the ulnar nerve in the left hand. Irritation of this nerve causes a *lump of scarlike tissue in the palm of the hand* (a nodule).

Although the nodules usually appear after the patient has suffered his heart attack, occasionally they will appear without the patient having known that he suffered a heart attack. In this case, the individual has suffered a *"silent heart attack."* After the silent heart attack occurs, the hand may become swollen. The swelling eventually subsides but a lump of hardened tissue may be left in the palm of the hand as evidence of the unsuspected heart attack. Naturally, the telltale evidence of a silent heart attack should warn of a larger, more damaging heart attack in the future. Measures should be taken to prevent a future heart attack by putting the person on an appropriate diet, advising him to avoid walking in cold winds without a breath mask, and to refrain from excessive exertion but to get exercise in moderation.

In Figure 19 (page 50) you can see the changes made in the palm print by the presence of a nodule under the skin. This is evident by the groove that is made on the print instead of the usual dermal ridge (Figure 20). This point was brought home to me by a 59-year-old woman I examined after a severe coronary occlusion had taken place.

The Presence of Nodules as a Warning

At that time I noticed that she had the indicated nodules present under the skin of her palm, and so I questioned her concerning her past history of heart attack. To her knowledge she had had none, but several years earlier she experienced an abnormally severe attack of stomach pain. Later, of course, she had not noticed the appearance of nodules and the pain had eventually gone away without medication or a physician's attendance. I believe that the heart attack she suffered could have been prevented had the nodules been discovered earlier and her "silent heart attack" noted for what it was—a warning of the second heart attack.

Nodules have been observed as occurring simultaneously with genuine heart attacks in which the patient survives. I had an experience with this phenomenon when I attended a 62-year-old man who suffered a classic coronary heart attack. He stayed in the hospital six weeks and was out of work for five months—a usual procedure in this type of heart attack. Two months after his heart attack I noticed nodules in his left palm for the first time. Since he had been a patient of mine for a long time, I was aware that this was a new sign and definitely associated with the heart attack he had suffered.

A Contrasting Example of Heart Disease Detected

In contrast to the last two cases whose palm prints showed definite signs of heart trouble, Figure 21 shows the normal palm print of an elderly woman who consulted me with severe chest pains which resembled those of a heart condition. I did an

CHANGES
IN THE
PALMAR RIDGES

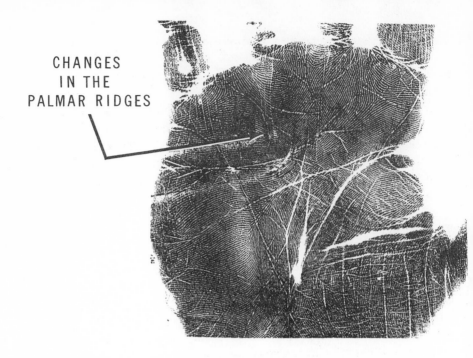

CHANGES
IN THE
PALMAR RIDGES

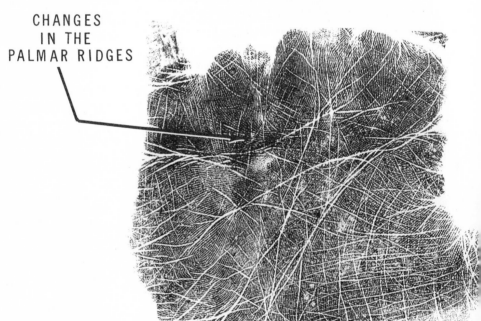

Figure 19. *Palm prints of two patients who have had coronary heart attacks. In both prints, the ridges in the area under the ring finger (the coronary area) are curved because of the nodules under the skin.*

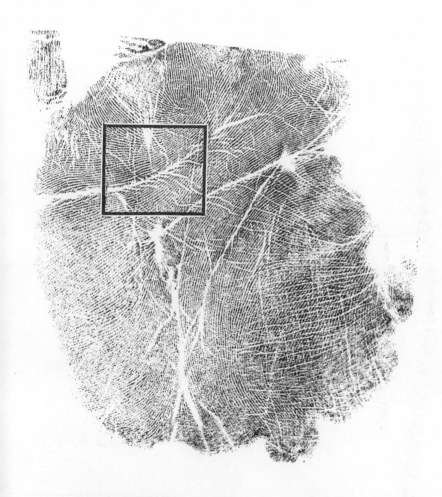

Figure 20. *Normal ridges in the coronary area.*

electrocardiogram on her and discovered minor coronary insufficiency. Naturally, I advised her to go to the hospital for further tests and bed rest. Much to my surprise, she refused to go
but wanted medicine to relieve the pain. I gave her medication
and the pain subsided the same day and never reappeared, except mildly after she had exerted herself too much. Now, 14
years later, this woman is still working—long past the age of
retirement—and appears to be going strong. She is as active and

vigorous as a much younger woman in good health would be. Evidently, her anxiety at this particular period in her life brought on mild heart spasms which subsided when she received the psychological assistance of medication during this crisis. As you can see in her palm print, the "coronary area" or the square that includes part of the heart line and the area under the ring finger is absolutely perfect. That is not the situation with the previous two cases. Their palm prints show defects in this area and their experience bore out the significance of these defects.

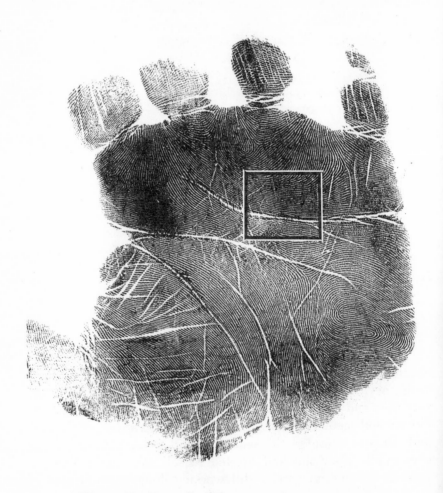

Figure 21. *Normal palm print in the coronary area.*

Indications of Internal and Mental Diseases

Schizophrenia, a commonly found form of mental illness, can be seen in the hand. According to Drs. A. Friedeman and Charlotte Wolff, abnormally long, externally flexible fingers and a palm with atrophied or shrunken muscles are suspicious signs of schizophrenia.

Glandular diseases are also associated with changes in the fingers and palm. The famed brain surgeon, Dr. Harvey Cushing, once stated that he could tell from the fingers alone if pituitary obesity in an individual started before or after adolescence. If pituitary obesity begins before adolescence, there will be fat pads on the back of the hand and the back of the second and third phalanges of the fingers. However the first phalange, at the tip of the finger, is slender or tapering. In adult pituitary obesity, which occurs after adolescence, there are no pads on the back of the hand and the fingers, and the fingertips do not taper.

Long, flexible fingers are also indicative of underdeveloped pituitary or sex glands. The fingers are usually very delicate and slender and there is no muscular shrinking in the palm.

Cretinism (idiocy) is recognizable because of a pronounced underdevelopment of the hand both functionally and morphologically. The hand of the cretin is broad and very short with stout fingers and spatulate tips. The fifth finger is short, pointed, and crooked. The thumb is short, ugly, and misshapen and there is a blunted, bulbous tip. Nail development is poor and the palms and fingers are covered with a dry, cold pallid, hard, and coarse skin which is rigid and causes impaired movement of the fingers. The muscle tone is poor and the use of the fingers is limited to awkward movements of the hand as a whole, rather than the purposeful movement of the individual digit. Early recognition of cretinism is the greatest service a palmist can perform for the parents of a child born with this condition. Prompt medical attention can bring about dramatic results in these individuals, and a human vegetable can be turned into a normal, functioning adult. Nothing is more gratifying, in my opinion, than to see one of these unfortunate children restored to humanity because of early diagnosis and correct treatment.

There are other signs indicating the presence of internal disease that change the appearance of the palm or fingers. But, we will describe only two other common diseases: diabetes and cancer.

Muscle atrophy, or muscle shrinking may occur in several diseases, sometimes before other symptoms appear. If shrinking occurs and there is no neurological disorder, diabetes may be present. Dr. Max Ellenberg[1], professor of Mount Sinai Medical

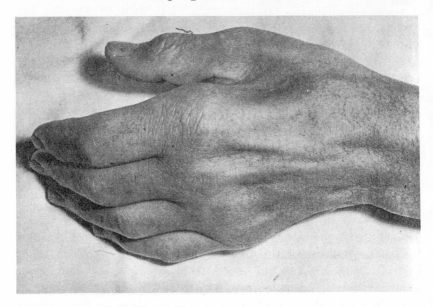

Figure 22. *Muscle shrinking of back of the hand at the base of the thumb and the index finger. Courtesy of Max Ellenberg, M.D., Journal of Mount Sinai Hospital, Vol. XXXV, No. 2, March-April, 1968.*

School in New York, stated that more than one out of every four diabetics show signs of muscle shrinking, frequently long before the appearance of the usual symptoms of diabetes mellitus. He observed that this muscle shrinking takes place primarily in the space between the thumb and the index finger (Figure 22) and on the base of the thumb and the little finger.

---

[1] "Diabetic Neuropathy of the Upper Extremities." *Journal of Mount Sinai Hospital*, Vol. XXXV, No. 2, March-April, 1968.

If an individual has this type of muscle shrinking or a physician notices this condition in a patient, the presence of diabetes should immediately be suspected even if no other symptoms have appeared.

One interesting aspect of the fingers and their relationship to disease is that each of the five fingers is associated with a different organic system of the body. Dr. Charlotte Wolff associates the thumb with vitality and the general state of health, the index finger with the respiratory system and the stomach, the middle finger with the liver and intestines, the ring finger with the kidney and the blood circulation, and the little finger with the feet and the sexual glands. She emphasized, however, that differential diagnosis depends on other signs present in the hand, particularly on the shape and quality of the nails. It would be wise for the individual who notices a serious abnormality in one of his fingers to suspect problems in the area associated with that particular finger. It would then be logical for him to consult a doctor who specializes in that area to confirm or deny the presence of disease. These preventive measures could quite possibly be the first step in heading off a serious condition. In any case, if there is an unusual feature in a particular finger, an individual should be alerted to the possible nature of his difficulty, and thereby be forewarned should any later symptoms arise.

Signs of Malignancy

About 20 years ago when I began to study palmistry, I visited a well-known palmist in New York. She called my attention to certain signs which are supposed to indicate the presence of cancer. I found it so incredible that I ignored her remarks and started to ask her questions about other aspects of palmistry.

A few years ago I was amazed when I learned from an editorial in the *Journal of the American Medical Association*[2] that palmar changes were observed in a large portion of patients with cancer. These alterations are called palmar keratoses. They are usually few in number and located mainly on the Mount of Venus (Figure

---

[2] December 20, 1965.

23) and the Mount of Luna, are pearly, yellow, or flesh-colored, and are translucent. Most patients are unaware of their presence inasmuch as the lesions are asymptomatic.

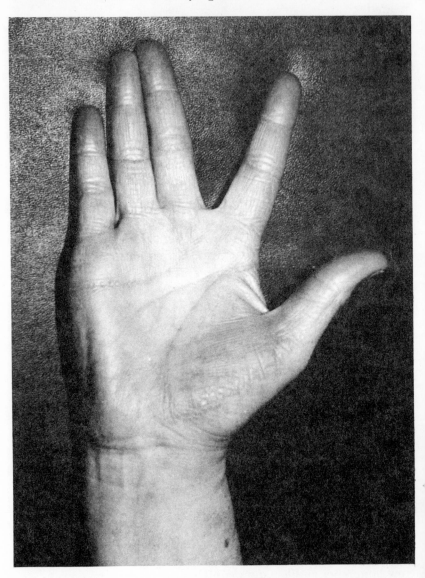

Figure 23. *Palmar keratoses on the Mount of Venus.*

Dr. R. L. Dobson[3] and his associates studied 671 patients with proved cancers. They found palmar keratoses in 46 per cent of the men and 26 per cent of the women. In a control of 685 persons without cancer, palmar keratoses were seen in only 12 per cent of the men and 5 per cent of the women.

These lesions were observed in all types of cancer. For example, palmar lesions were found in 54 per cent of the men with cancer of the skin, 45 per cent with cancer of the lung, and 44 per cent with cancer of the colon.

Since the presence of palmar keratoses may indicate the presence of some type of cancer, the lesion should be looked for diligently in all patients and regarded conscientiously if found. Although prospective studies will be necessary to determine whether palmar keratoses have any screening value, perhaps medical palmistry will provide a simple means of detecting some patients with early cancer.

Dr. Richard C. Gible[4] emphasized that a chest roentgenogram should be taken when diffuse keratosis of the palms appears in otherwise apparently healthy persons to see if there is lung cancer.

In the last two years, I studied the palm of 42 patients with all types of cancer and found that 16 had palmar lesions.

Now the question arises, what should you do when you recognize these very significant signs? *Do not diagnose cancer.* You should not even mention that you are concerned about the signs in your subject's palm. Continue analyzing his hand, discuss other aspects of his health and personality, and then ask him the following questions which are cancer's warning signals:

1. Do you have unusual bleeding or discharge?
2. A lump or thickening in the breast or elsewhere?
3. A sore that does not heal?
4. Change in bowel or bladder habits?
5. Persistent hoarseness or cough?

---

[3] *Archives of Dermatology,* November, 1965.
[4] "Alterations of Palm and Soles — Indicators of Internal Disease," *N.Y. State Journal of Medicine,* May, 1965.

6. Persistent indigestion or difficulty in swallowing?

7. Change in a wart or mole?

If the subject answers affirmatively to any of the questions, then you should refer him to a physician. But try not to alarm him. Encourage him to have a physical checkup and watch his health closely for the next few years. If he wants to know why, tell him his palm indicates possible illness.

If your subject follows your advice and three years later findings are negative, forget the palmar keratoses.

8

The Significance of Ridge
Patterns of Palm and Fingers

The most scientific and recent area of study in medical palmistry is that of the ridge patterns of the palm and fingers. This new area of study is called "dermatoglyphics." These marks or "skin carvings," as one researcher calls them, develop in the first four months of a child's life in the womb, when the fetus is most susceptible to viral or other harmful conditions.

Students of dermatoglyphics believe that if these negative or unhealthy environmental factors interfere with the growth of the child in the womb, they later not only cause congenital diseases (such as heart defects, mental and neurological disorders, schizophrenia, and so on) but also create abnormal palm print patterns.

In the last ten years, more than 200 scientific papers have been published on this subject. Dr. James R. Miller of the Children's Hospital in Vancouver, British Columbia, who evaluated 1,000 school children, urges that the study of dermatoglyphics be a part of a child's routine examination, because it provides information which might at times be critical in making or confirming a diagnosis of abnormal mental or physical development. Many other researchers agree with him.

Observing Hand Prints

One of the greatest advantages of palm print studies is that they are easily available and cost nothing. The smear test from the mouth, the so-called karyotyping, is very expensive and relatively few laboratories can give this type of test. According to Dr. James B. Thompson of the University of Toronto, dermatoglyphic studies may establish diagnosis in doubtful cases without karyotyping. In an editorial in the December 8, 1966 issue of *The New England Journal of Medicine,* dermatoglyphics was called "the poor man's karyotype."

In most individuals, skin patterns can be observed with a simple magnifying glass in good, direct lighting; but, to obtain a permanent record or to do some research, I would advise you to take palm prints. The best methods to obtain a palm print are fingerprint sets used by the police or the FBI. You may ask them where you may obtain a set or you may find firms in the telephone directory in your city.*

At this point, I should like to remind my readers that the science of dermatoglyphics is still in its infancy, despite the fact that more articles have been published on this subject than on the rest of medical palmistry as a whole. It is still a complicated science and in some respects it is not conclusive. Therefore, only a scientist who specializes in genetics or constitutional medicine could truly comprehend it. However, any layman or a palmist who is interested in better health, should be acquainted with the basic principles of dermatoglyphics to gain additional information about certain medical problems.

For the beginner, I would suggest learning about the following three basic factors in the study of fingers and palm prints.

---

* One firm is Fingerprint Equipment Laboratory, 5526 N. Elston Avenue, Chicago, Illinois.

(Each will be discussed in turn under their respective headings below.)

1. The formation, frequency, and location of the ridge patterns.

2. The location of the axial triradius and the degrees of triradius angle.

3. The ridge count.

The Ridge Patterns

There are five main fingerprint patterns: loops, arches, whorls, composites, and tented types.

1. Of these types the loop is the most common. It has a center or core and a triangle which is called a triradius (Figure 24).

Figure 24. *The loop type.*

2. The arch is, as the name implies, a plain arch. It has a simple pattern and, unlike the loop, has no triradius (Figure 25).

Figure 25. *The arch type.*

3. The whorl is a design where the majority of ridges makes a circle around the core or hub. It has two triradii (Figure 26).

Figure 26. *The whorl type.*

4. Composites compound designs of two or more patterns, usually of twin loops, which run in an adverse way (Figure 27).

Figure 27. *The composite type.*

5. The tented types (sometimes called tented arches) are characterized by vertical elevation of the horizontal ridges, re-

Figure 28. *The tented type.*

sembling a tent and, contrary to the plain arches, often have a triradius (Figure 28).

All five patterns occur also in the palm on the base of the middle and ring finger, and on the Mounts of Luna and Venus, scientifically known as the hypothenar and the thenar eminence.

Triradius

The triradii in the palm are more significant than those which are associated with fingerprint patterns. There are two types: (1) the digital triradii are known as A, B, C, and D, located on the bases of the second, third, fourth, and fifth fingers; (2) the axial triradius, known as T, is located normally at the base of the palm between the Mounts of Luna and Venus.

Lines drawn from the A and D triradii to the axial triradius form what is known as the ATD angle. See Figs. 29-a and 29-b (pages 64 and 65).

The Ridge Count

We will discuss only two important counts: (1) loop ridge count on the finger from the triradial point to the core (Figures 30a, and 30b) and (2) A-B ridge count on the palm (Figure 31).

To count accurately, you must have a magnifying glass and a long needle. Most importantly though, you must count along a straight line.

We shall evaluate the basics of dermatoglyphics in relation to congenital abnormalities.

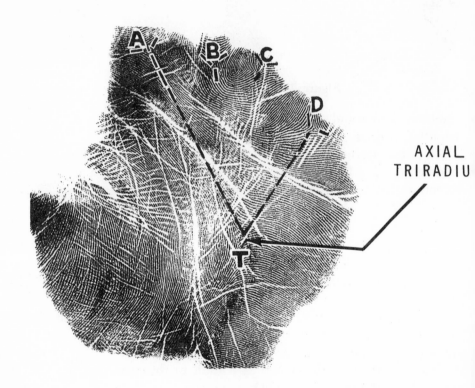

AXIAL
TRIRADIU

Figure 29-a. *Displaced axial triradius, wide ATD angle.*

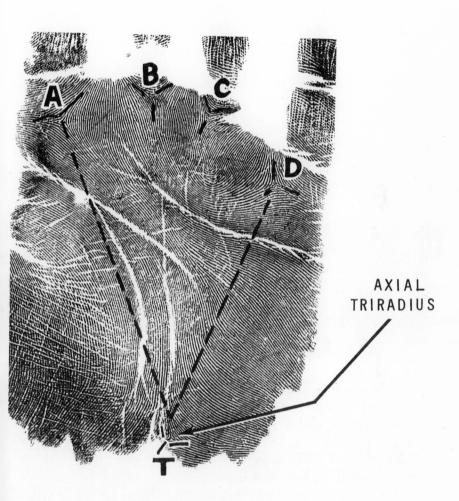

Figure 29-b. *Normally placed axial triradius, normal degree ATD angle.*

Figure 30-a. *The normal loop ridge count is 12.*

Figure 30-b. *Low ridge count, in this case 8.*

In order to simplify and not confuse you, try to remember only the following factors:

1. In a normal hand, the loops and whorls are found more frequently on the fingers, and arches and tented types are most common on the palm. Therefore, if you find arches on the fingers and loops or whorls on the palm, you know that there is something unusual concerning the heredity of the individual and should begin further investigation.

2. In the average hand there are no patterns on the Mount of Luna or on the Mount of Venus except on the base of the fingers. If you find patterns on the mounts, consider it an additional sign of genetic alteration.

3. Monkeys have patterns of the same type on all ten fingers. This is a simian or animalistic trait and hands such as these are called monomorphic hands. According to many observers, only 10 to 20 per cent of all human beings have monomorphic hands

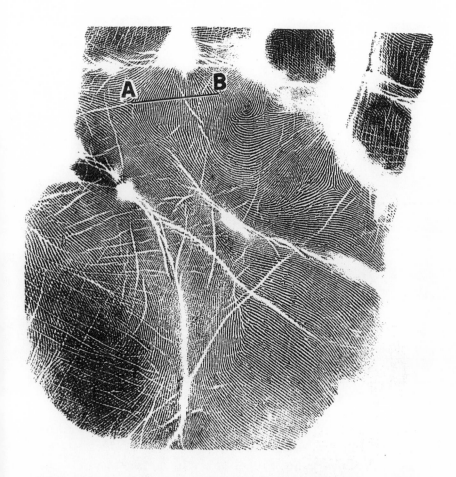

Figure 31. *A and B triradii. The normal A-B ridge count, as shown here, is 34.*

(Figure 32). Dr. C. Wolff concluded that monomorphic hands have simian characteristics, pointing to an abnormality of some kind in a person with hands of this type.

4. The normal degree of the ATD angle is around 45 degrees.

5. In the normal hand, the average loop ridge count is 12 to 14 and the AB ridge count is 34.

If you find three of the five factors abnormal, you may conclude that the person has some congenital defects.

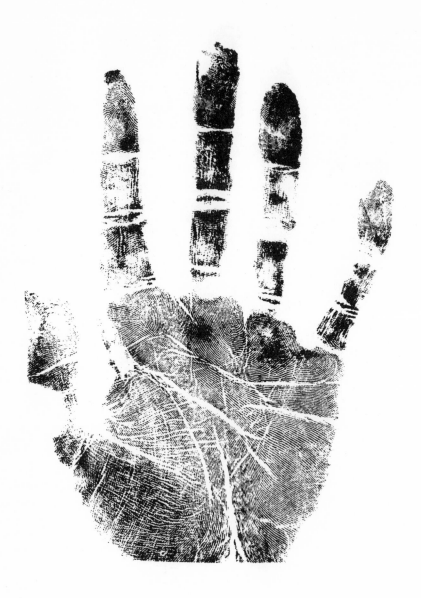

Figure 32. *Monomorphic hands; loop type patterns on all ten fingers.*

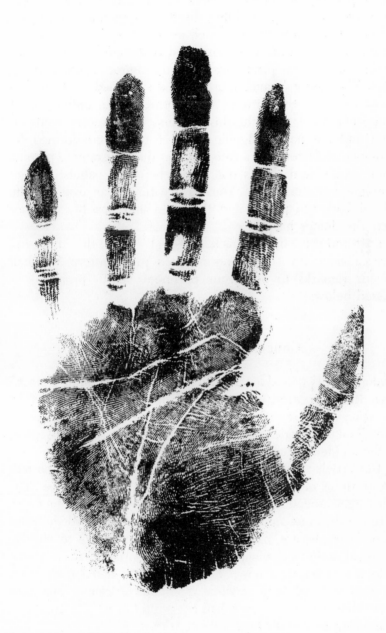

The types of congenital diseases which can be seen in the hand range from such disabling diseases as mental retardation to simple correctable diseases such as neurosis. In the study of a person's hand you must keep in mind that there are two major ways in which palm prints are formed—environmental and inherited. The parents' hands must also be examined to determine the way in which the patterns were formed in an individual. If the subject's hands resemble his parents', the patterns were inherited and are not as significant as if they were formed by environmental factors. As a rule, doctors do not examine parents or their hands, and this is one area where the palmist has an advantage over the doctor. You, as a palmist, can examine the hands of both the parent and the child and possibly discover defects the doctor has not.

It is beyond the scope of this text to deal with all the congenital diseases associated with an abnormal palm print pattern. We shall limit our remarks to only four pertinent health problems as discussed below.

Congenital Heart Diseases

Under the title, "Sudden Death Traced to Congenital Defect," a news item appeared in the *Journal of the American Medical Association* which said that unsuspected congenital abnormalities of the coronary arteries may occasionally be found in individuals who die suddenly during physical exertion.

In this article, seven instances of sudden death were reported; three of these individuals died after a long distance race. The victims' ages ranged from 11 to 27 years. The significant factor is, "There had been no signs or symptoms pointing toward the presence of heart disease and the subject had been able to indulge in physical activities." Chances are, the majority of those young people would be alive now, *if someone had taken their palm print and warned them against strenuous exercise.* The post mortem showed that all seven had congenital heart abnormalities.

According to the medical palmist, the majority of congenital heart ailments leave imprints in the palm. Drs. T. Takashina and S. Yorifuji reported in an article in the *Journal of the American*

Medical Association[1] titled, "Palmar Dermatoglyphics in Heart Disease" that the frequency of displacement of the palmar axial triradii in either hand occurred with significantly greater frequency in patients with congenital heart disease (64 per cent) than in patients with "acquired" heart disease (17 per cent).

Rubella Syndrome

Much has been written about the fact that if a pregnant mother contracts German measles (rubella) her child may be affected with a congenital disease called rubella syndrome. After the birth, a mother who has had rubella will be in constant fear that her child is abnormal. You might help relieve her anxiety if you study her child's palm.

According to Dr. Milton Alter of the University of Minnesota, the children who suffer from this syndrome differ from the normal child in having a higher frequency of whorls on the fingers, a reduced AB ridge count, a wider ATD angle, and a tendency toward more patterns on the palm.

Sex Chromosomal Deviations from Normal Patterns

The study of dermatoglyphics could help us solve and prevent some abnormal sexual behavior, especially in reference to masculinity and femininity. A great many individuals retain some remnant of bisexuality, and in some instances it could cause certain difficulties for these persons in their relation to the opposite sex. In certain chromosomal abnormalities the bisexuality or ambisexuality is so predominant that it delays or prevents the development of certain secondary sexual characteristics. The most important disorders of this nature are the so-called Turner and Klinefelter syndromes.

In Turner's syndrome the person is a female who looks like a male, and the person who has Klinefelter syndrome is a male who has some feminine characteristics. Usually these conditions cannot be recognized until after puberty when the secondary sexual features are poorly developed. Very often these patients seek professional advice when it is too late for a doctor to help them.

---

[1] August 29, 1966.

Examination of the finger and palm prints of a child could give you a clue to such a disorder before puberty. You should know the signs and if you recognize them, you could be extremely helpful by recommending a sex-chromatic analysis by a doctor.

You could help prevent development of serious psycho-social problems in a teen-age girl who becomes aware that her breasts are not developed, or that she has not menstruated. The same applies to a boy who is told that his sex organ is small and his breasts are too big. Remember, if the diagnosis is made early enough, these individuals could be given satisfactory hormone therapy by a physician.

Many fingerprint patterns have a different incidence of occurrence in persons with Turner and Klinefelter syndromes than they have in normal subjects.

Dr. Anne Forbes, a professor at Harvard Medical School, observed[2] that loops constituted 81 and 54 per cent of the patterns on the right thumb and middle fingers, respectively, as compared with 56 and 32 per cent in the general population. They were less frequent on the fifth fingers, where whorls were correspondingly increased to 25 and 33 per cent on the right and left hands as compared to 11.4 and 6.9 per cent of the general population. She also found on the Mount of Luna 15 per cent of certain composites resembling the letter "s" in comparison with 3 per cent in normal subjects.

In Klinefelter syndrome there are two significant dermatoglyphic traits: an increase of arches in all fingers and a low ridge count. Dr. Forbes stated that the most striking difference between the hands of the patient with Klinefelter syndrome and the normal person is the ridge count on right index fingers. The average count of these fingers was 8.5 in contrast to the normal average for all fingers of 14.5 for males and 12.5 for females. At this point, I would like to emphasize again that you cannot depend on one sign, or as a matter of fact on dermatoglyphic characteristics alone, you must look for other signs also.

In some sex chromosomal aberrations, especially in females, there are additional important features such as puffiness of the

---

[2] Forbes, A., *New England Journal of Medicine*, December 8, 1966.

hand, underdeveloped nails, and a short, incurved little finger which is usually widely separated from the ring finger.

Constitutional Neurosis

The fate of a "born neurotic" depends a great deal on his relation to his mother and his early environmental experiences. If he is neglected and unwanted by his mother or his environmental conditions are unfavorable, his neurotic tendencies will provide a fertile ground for development of neurotic conflicts.

The study of dermatoglyphics could help you recognize constitutional tendencies toward neurosis in a child. If you do, you could advise his mother to give the child plenty of love and attention in the first few years of his life.

I did an extensive study of the palm print of hereditary neurotics and found the following abnormal dermatoglyphic features:

1. Displaced axial triradius (See Figure 29-a on page 64.);
2. Whorls or loops on the Mount of Luna (Figure 33) (page 74).
3. An increase of composite on all fingers and on the Mount of Venus;
4. Disassociated or ill-formed ridges known as "Strings of Pearls" (Figure 34).

I must emphasize again that these patterns are indicative only of a *predisposition* to neurosis.

I would like to end this chapter with the same conclusion as did Drs. H. Cummins and C. Midlo in their classic, *Fingerprints, Palms and Soles*,[3] page 280:

> "In its broadest scope, dactylomancy (reading fingerprints) extends to the reading of past, present and future, as in the similar pseudo-science of palmistry. To the extent that dactylomancy concerns itself with a search for signs of constitutional makeup it merits attention as genuine scientific inquiry. As an object of investigation, this is not so far-fetched as it may seem to be at first thought. Since flexion creases and dermatoglyphics vary in other constitutional expression,

---

[3] Dover Publication Inc., New York, 1961.

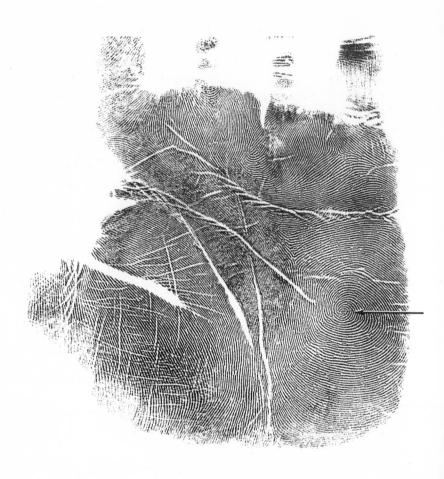

Figure 33. *Whorl on the Mount of Luna.*

a correlation between dermatoglyphics and the character-temperament constitution may be ultimately demonstrated."

They quote certain Japanese experts who state that the finger patterns often indicate certain personality traits. They cite the whorl, which signifies stubbornness—the loop, which signifies a lack of perseverance—and the arches, which signify a cruel and merciless character.

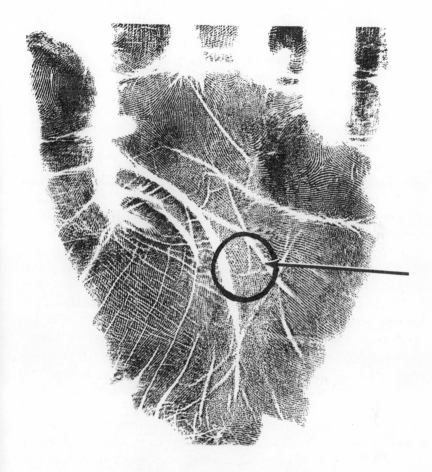

Figure 34. *"Strings of Pearls."*

Indications of Fingerprint Patterns

My own observation has led me to feel that fingerprint patterns often indicate certain characteristics. At times they correspond with those listed by the famous London palmist, Noel Jaquin. To associate fingerprint patterns to personality traits you must consider the patterns which constitute the majority in all ten fingers. If six or more fingerprints are of the loop type, the person is adaptable, has mental and emotional elasticity, and a tendency to be easygoing; perhaps he even is a little too responsive to the moods of others. Being versatile, a person such as this often finds it difficult to concentrate on one subject at a time.

A rundown on a tented-type person sounds surprisingly like the astrological description of an individual born under the sign of Libra. Sensitive to every stimulus, he is strongly influenced by his environment and easily gets out of balance. He is also idealistic, and is responsive to peace, harmony, and beauty. Often he is interested in music and the other arts.

A person with composites can be characterized by vacillation. His fingerprints show two loops running in opposite directions—as often the mind of this kind of person does. He finds it difficult to form definite opinions and conclusions. At times he shows executive ability, but his potential cannot be realized unless he can achieve self-control and a single direction of goal. The person must make up his mind as to what he wants and where he wants to go.

The arch type betrays a basic mistrust, not only of others but also of himself. He always questions his own actions and the wisdom of his decisions. As a person with this type of pattern grows older he becomes introspective through his anxiety to avoid error.

The whorl type is probably the most important of all the patterns. The keynote of this type is individuality. The subject is independent, determined, and original. He acts and thinks for himself. He can be influenced only by logic and conventional mores. He may be a criminal, a rebel, and/or a radical—perhaps a beatnik. However, the constructive defier is the person who goes on to excel in the sciences and arts, unaffected either by convention or opposition. Einstein was a whorl-type individual.

If no pattern makes up the majority in all ten fingers, then consider the pattern of the thumb as an indicator. If you find a discrepancy between the pattern of the thumbs and the predominant patterns in the fingers, you may suspect that the person has a combination of characteristic traits.

To evaluate such a person you have to analyze the whole hand, especially the most revealing diagnostic signs, the chiroglyphics—the lines and the marks of the palm.

9

Palm Lines and Markings

In the previous chapters, we discussed only one aspect of the palm prints, the pattern of the dermal ridges. In this chapter we shall begin to study the most important part of palmistry, the lines and markings of the palm.

To differentiate these lines and markings from the dermal ridges, we shall call them *chiroglyphics*. We classify them into three groups: 1. Flexion creases; 2. Accessory lines; and 3. Symbols (sometimes called accidental signs).

The flexion creases, which are located at the joints, are directly related to the movement of the joints. The accessory lines are only indirectly associated with flexion of the hands, and the symbols have no relation to movements of the joints. The symbols, according to many students, are like the fingerprints—signs of identification of an individual. In the words of Aristotle, "The lines are not written into the human hands without reason, they come from heavenly influences and man's own individuality." We shall discuss the symbols and accessory lines in more detail in later chapters.

Flexion Creases

There are three flexion creases which are related to our health:
the thenar line (known as the line of life) and the lower and
upper transverse lines (known as the line of head and the line
of heart) (Figure 35).

They reflect, respectively, our physical, mental, and emotional
health. These flexion creases are formed at the same time during
the third and fourth fetal months (child development in the
womb) as the ridge patterns. As Dr. J. S. Thompson in his book,
Genetic Medicine, pointed out, they are determined in part by
the same forces that affect ridge alignment; therefore, it is logical
to assume that the forces causing congenital aberration (defects)
and abnormal ridge patterns also could produce abnormal crease
lines. To prove this assumption, I would like to introduce one of
the most revealing genetic signs, the *simian crease line,* which is
the most characteristic crease in the hands of monkeys. The
simian line is a very common feature in the hands of persons
with congenital and chromosomal disorders.

In a significant article, "The Single Transverse Palmar-Crease
in Infants and Children" (*Develop. Med. Child. Neurology 1965,*
5-491), Drs. P. A. Davies and V. Smallpeice stated, "Few clini-
cians will have time to master the intricacies of dermal ridge
patterns, but the presence of a single transverse crease (syn-
onyms: simian crease, four finger line) can be seen at a glance.
The association of such a crease with mongolism has been known
for some time, but it is not so widely appreciated that it may
be found with other abnormalities, as well as in normal people."
They reported that *abnormalities of the central nervous system
were most commonly associated with the simian line,* and also
mentioned a wide range of other abnormalities; for example,
Thalidomide drug damage in infants.

Because of its importance, we shall deal with the simian line
in a separate chapter. In this chapter, we shall only evaluate
those crease lines which are closely associated with diseases.

To emphasize the significance of flexion creases, I should like
to repeat their relation to ridge patterns by quoting Drs. Davies
and Smallpeice, "Although the flexion creases are not considered

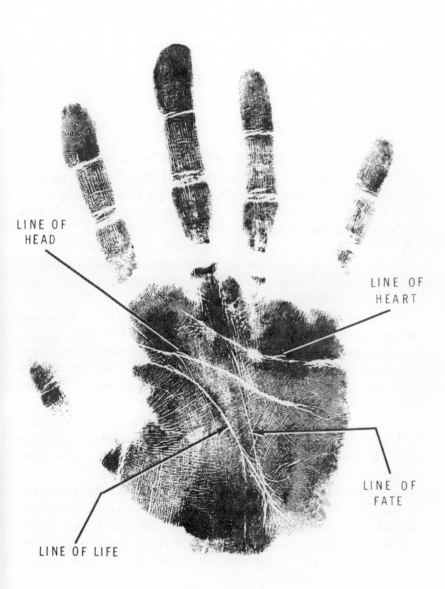

Figure 35. *Flexion creases.*

elements of dermatoglyphics, there must inevitably be close association between the two."

Because flexion crease lines and ridge patterns are closely related, we could state that, if abnormal dermatoglyphic traits are the imprints of disease, the ill-formed flexion creases could also be indications of abnormal health disorders.

The Life Line (Thenar Line)

In relation to our health, the palm's life line is by far the most important line to consider. It is associated with the movement of the most vital digit of men, the thumb. It begins between the thumb and the base of the index finger and encircles the Mount of Venus (the thenar eminence).

The life line is the mirror of our health, vitality, and constitution. That is the reason why some palmists erroneously associate the strength and length of the life line with the longevity of our life.

As a medical doctor, I have known many patients who died young despite their long and well-developed life lines. I have also met many people who reached old age despite their short and weak life lines. Therefore, perhaps the most appropriate name for this crease should be the *line of constitution.*

A long, deep, well-marked line is a sign of strong vitality and constitution; whereas, the short, thin, faulty line is an imprint of a weak and delicate constitution with little or no vitality. Persons with the latter type of line have less power to endure and resist diseases or injuries.

In the majority of cases, you will observe that the beginning of the life line is chained or poorly marked, indicating that these persons, like most of us, had childhood diseases. If the rest of the line is deep, well-formed, and unbroken, you could assume that the childhood diseases strengthened their resistance and immunity to other ailments.

If you find a broken life line in your palm, don't come to any conclusion without considering other equally revealing signs of impending diseases. It should be noted here that faulty crease lines like abnormal ridge patterns not only develop during fetal growth as a result of disease conditions but are also passed on genetically from the parents and have no diagnostic significance.

Significance of a Broken Life Line

In a majority of cases you could consider a broken life line as a warning signal—danger ahead—so, be more health-minded, try to avoid all factors that could damage your health such as smoking, overstraining, and overeating; when you develop a symptom such as pain or loss of appetite, consult your physician. As an example of this, an acquaintance of mine asked me to read her palm one day. She wanted to know whether I would come to the same conclusions as another palmist did. He told her that her life line was broken; therefore, in the near future she would have an accident or a serious illness.

I reassured her that no one could predict the future or make any kind of prognosis by any one sign alone, and told her that there was no other sign in her palm which signified an abnormal condition; therefore, she should ignore that one particular sign. However, I advised her that during the next four years if anything unusual occurred, to consult her doctor promptly.

About eight months later the woman called me. She proceeded to tell me that a few weeks earlier she began to worry about her menstrual period because it had lasted longer than usual. At that time she made an appointment to see her gynecologist—three days hence. However, the next day she developed sudden pain and insisted the doctor see her at once. He did and fortunately was able to diagnose an extra-uterine pregnancy and operated on her immediately. After the operation he remarked to her, "How very fortunate that you came to see me because your tubal pregnancy ruptured just one-half hour before the operation."

This woman's parents did not have a broken life line. If they had, this sign in her hand would have been no indication of impending danger in her life. Since her parents' palms were different from hers in this respect, I interpreted the broken life line in her hand as a warning signal.

Islands on the Life Line

In addition to the break on the life line, you should also look for an island. According to the traditional interpretation of the palmist, the island is a sign of impending disease or a dangerous health period. Sorell concluded, in his very interesting book on the hand, that an egg-shaped island on the life line is a sign of oncoming cancer. I have seen the hands of only two people with cancer since Sorell's book was published. One did not have an island. I had taken the palm print of the other several years ago, and after cancer was discovered, I again looked at her hand and found the sign of an island (Figure 36).

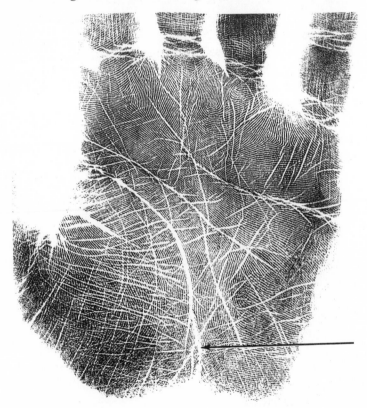

Figure 36. *Palm print of a patient with terminal cancer. Note large island at the end of the life line.*

The Head Line (Lower Transverse Line)

The head line is closely related to the life line. It starts at the same place as the life line and it also is a chart of our health.

The life line reflects our general health and constitution, and the head line denotes our mental health. According to many observers, an ill-formed or a broken head line is a signal of impending nervous or mental breakdown.

If you have such a break in your head line, you should learn to avoid mental strain, excitement, and aggravation. In extreme cases you may need a sedative, in mild cases you may need the tranquilizing effect of art and music to find a release or escape for your nervous and sensitive constitution.

Dr. Charlotte Wolff studied the palms of 650 mentally defective patients and an equal number of normal subjects. She found that 70 per cent of the mentally defective patients had faulty or broken head lines as compared to 30 per cent in normal persons. She also observed that abnormally short head lines were a very common feature in the low-grade, mentally defective person.

The Heart Line (Upper Transverse Line)

A person who is physically or mentally ill is usually emotionally disturbed; therefore, to evaluate the health connotation of both the life line and the head line you have to learn to interpret another significant flexion crease—the line of the heart.

In our age of anxiety, perhaps one could state, as many palmists do, that the heart line is the most vital one of all. It is often indicative, as the name implies, of our greatest emotional and physical trauma—the "broken heart" and the damaged heart. Many people become sick, commit suicide, and kill others because of disappointment in love and many millions die young because of heart failure.

In this chapter, we shall deal only with the diagnostic value of the heart line in reference to cardiac diseases.

Again, I should like to advise my readers, don't diagnose heart ailments. Only a physician with the aid of a stethoscope, x-ray, cardiogram, and physical examination can do it. There were some famous palmists who could recognize heart ailments from the hand, but even they experienced difficulties.

In referring to these difficulties William C. Benham,[1] the most quoted palmist said, "You will constantly be called upon to judge whether some marking seen on a heart line is a health defect, an event in the life, or an indication of character, and this is a point which has puzzled many excellent practitioners."

He advised that to find out whether an ill-formed or broken heart line is an indication of heart ailment, one should study the nails and the life line.

To make a diagnosis, Benham said that one should see if the nails are clubbed and the base of the nails are blue. If either or both of these signs are present, you can suspect heart disease. Then, he continues, check the unevenness in the life line; does it split or break, or is it crossed? Is there a line that runs from the defect on the heart line to the life line?

"Not finding," as Benham concluded, "any of these health defects, it is evident the mark on the heart line is one showing some characteristic of the affections and not disease."

I observed that the nodules which occur in coronary heart disease (See Figure 19 in Chapter 7) are associated with an island on the heart line. Therefore, if you find any kind of defect (such as a break, a chain, or an island) on the heart line below the little finger or ring finger, consider it a possible sign of disease, especially if the individual also exhibits certain contributory factors to coronary disease—such as anxiety, overweight, high cholesterol, and high blood pressure. Remind the person of the heart line defect and advise him to take it easy and slow down.

The significance of both the island on the heart line and the island on the life line has never been proven or disproven scientifically. As far as I know, research of this type is not done anywhere, and perhaps the interpretation of these islands by some palmists is a fallacy. Fallacy or not, if you are responsible for a person having a regular, routine physical examination because you have found this sign in his hand, this fallacy, just as a placebo, is an essential part of the art of healing.

---

[1] *The Laws of Scientific Hand Reading*, Duell, Sloan and Pearce, New York, 1900, p. 408.

II

HAND PSYCHOLOGY

10

The Analysis of "Signatures" of the Hand

Our medical ancestors believed that certain hand features are not only imprints of disease but also reflections of the total nature of their patients—their body, mind, and soul. They believed as stated in the bible, "He sealeth up the hand of every man; that all men may know his work" (Job:37:7).

This concept assumed a great importance in the 15th and 16th centuries in the so-called doctrine of signatures—an organized body of knowledge which showed a reasoned connection between illness and therapeutic results.

Dr. Lester King,[1] senior editor of the *Journal of the American Medical Association,* explained clearly and beautifully the meaning which this doctrine had to physicians of the Middle Ages in an article entitled "The Road to Scientific Therapy."

---

[1] *J.A.M.A.,* July 25, 1966, Vol. 197, No. 4.

According to the theory of the doctrine of signatures, certain qualities or potentialities inherent in humans, animals, and every growing, living thing could be recognized from certain signs or forms. For example, we could, from a sign or shape, differentiate a poisonous snake or mushroom from a nonpoisonous one. Dr. King stated that the adherent of the doctrine of signatures believed that man possessed a soul and reason. The lower animals lacked these but possessed certain divine properties imbedded in their material form—various powers, virtues, and potentialities.

The soul is the form of man and we learn the characteristics of the human soul by careful study of external features and actions. In lower creatures, we can identify intrinsic powers and virtues by carefully observing the material house or shell.

Dr. King stated, "In humans the study of physiognomy can tell a great deal about the personality . . . the appearance and behavior of the body represents the sign—the signature—of the soul."

However, the important thing that we must know, as Dr. King pointed out, is ". . . where to look, what sign to observe— we must be able to *read* the signature." What could be more revealing than the form and gestures of the human hand, and most important, the signs and markings of the palm?

So far we have dealt mainly with certain hand features in relation to physical diseases. From now on we shall concentrate on the psychological aspect of our health and well-being.

We shall try to learn something about our character, temperament and personality from the shape of the hand and the markings of the palm. In doing so, we may understand certain medical problems which cannot be cured by modern surgery or by modern miracle drugs.

Signature Analysis Areas of the Hand

To analyze the "signature" of the hand in reference to the totality of an individual we shall divide the hand into different parts. I prefer the vertical division suggested by Dr. C. Wolff because it includes not only the palm but also the fingers. According to Dr. Wolff, the first zone comprises the thumb, the thenar eminence (Mount of Venus), the index finger, and the palm beneath it. This is called the radial zone. This part of the hands reflects our ego or conscious mind and our relation to the external world.

The second zone is on the opposite side of the hand and includes the little finger, the ring finger, the hypothenar eminence (Mount of Luna), and the palm below the little and ring fingers. This is called the ulnar zone and represents the "id" or unconscious aspects of our life, our imagination, our intuition or instinct, and our unconscious urges and tensions.

The third zone lies between these two and comprises the middle finger and the hollow of the palm. It is called the middle zone, which is the mirror of our conscious or unconscious conscience, the superego, the moderator between our conscious and unconscious tension.

In this chapter, we shall begin to evaluate the psychological connotations of some of the chiroglyphics. The palm print pattern is determined in a majority of cases at conception by the genes one inherits and is modified, and in certain respects changed, by environmental factors during fetal development and later during childhood growth.

Dr. J. A. Fraser Roberts, a professor at London University, explained the close relation between genes, heredity, and hand features in his book, *An Introduction to Medical Genetics*, by discussing in detail a congenital malformation of the nail, so-called anonychia. This malformation is characterized by the absence of the nails of the first three fingers and is due to the presence of an abnormal gene inherited from the parents. Dr. Roberts concluded that, if a person with anonychia marries a person without it, chances are that 50 per cent of their children will be affected; however, the normal children of affected parents will have only normal offspring if they marry persons without anonychia.

It should be noted by the reader that anonychia has no medical significance. This nail malformation does not cause any special problem. If a woman is concerned about it, she could wear artificial nails.

There are some congenital configurations of the hand which have more diagnostic significance; for example, polydactyly (more than five fingers) or syndactyly (joined or webbed fingers). These hereditary configurations are found in association with congenital heart disease and with some forms of mental retardation. The most important factor about the genes we inherit is that they could give us the same characteristics as our parents.

Dr. Walter Alvarez, the noted author and physician, stated in one of his lectures that he inherited certain characteristics and genes from his father because he had the same vein formation in the back of his hand as his father.

How to Trace Inherited Traits

If you compare some of the chiroglyphics of your palm with the palms of your parents or children, you could find out what kind of psychological traits you inherited from your parents and those you will give to your children.

The three palm prints shown in Figure 37 of a father, his daughter, and his grandson are good illustrations of the interrelation between genes, chiroglyphics, and personality traits. The head line of these prints has a *similar beginning and ending*, signifying that they all have similarity in certain behavior patterns. To evaluate these prints we must discuss other features of the head line.

Figure 37. *Palm prints of a man (top), his daughter (center), and his grandson (bottom) showing that the head line starts at the same point in each hand (left arrow). There is also a forked head line in each hand (right arrow). See opposite page.*

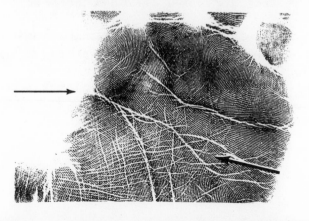

The head line is one of the most important "signatures" of the personality. It is a mirror of our mentality, our power of reason, concentration, and learning. It also reflects our attitude toward life, our fellowman, and our environment.

A good head line is relatively long, well-marked, unbroken, and slopes slightly toward the Mount of Luna (Figure 38). If you have such a line, you are practical, imaginative, and have a good mind and memory. If your head line runs straight and ends at the base of the little finger (Figure 39), you are very practical, materialistic, possessive, and often cold and emotionless.

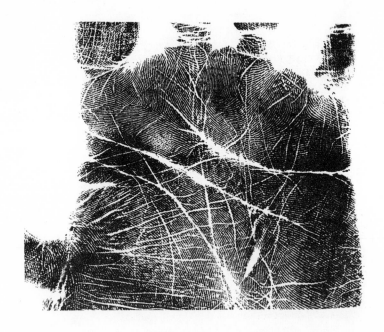

Figure 38. *Long, well-marked, and unbroken head line.*

If it slopes down too much, you are sentimental, sensitive, and an extremely imaginative person who has a tendency to escape from reality through daydreams and fantasy (Figure 40).

The degree of sloping often determines the attitude a person has toward the realities of life. If your head line ends close to the base of the palm, you will be prone to be withdrawn from

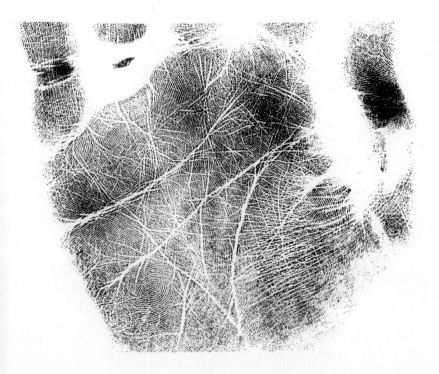

Figure 39. *Very long, straight head line ending at the base of the little finger.*

everyday life, even to the point of suicidal tendencies.

If your life line ends in a fork, as seen in the three palms in Figure 37 previously, you will have a versatile mentality which will enable you not only to dream but also, and more importantly, to make your dreams become a reality. That is why this type of head line is sometimes considered a sign of genius. Professor Einstein had such a head line.

The normal head line is joined to the life line at its starting point (Figure 41). If the lines remain joined for more than half an inch, it signifies caution and prudence; people with such palms consider the consequences of every step before taking it (Figure 42-a).

Shyness is also indicated if the two lines are united at the beginning point and are chained (Figure 42-b).

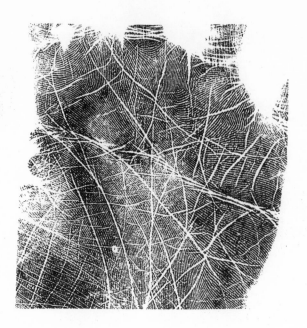

Figure 40. *Head line sloping downward, signifying sensitivity and strong imagination.*

Figure 41. *Normal starting point of head line and life line.*

Figure 42-a. *Abnormal starting point of head line. The head line and life line are joined for more than one-half inch. Palm print of pessimistic girl who is always cautious.*

Figure 42-b. *Chained union of head and life lines, indicating shyness.*

If the head line is completely separated from the life line at the root, it indicates impulsiveness, even recklessness; the greater the separation, the more prominent are these traits (Figure 43).

One may find not only the life line and the head line united at the root but also the heart line (Figure 44). This, say some palmists, is an unfavorable sign which signifies confusion of reason, emotion, and instinct. Others say it is a sign of immaturity and bad temper.

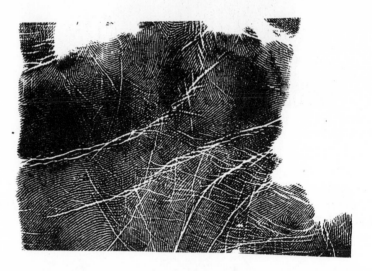

Figure 43. *This is a palm print of an impulsive and unpredictable female. The head line and life line are widely separated.*

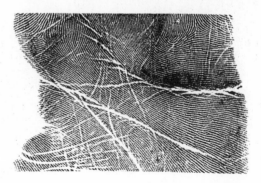

Figure 44. *The three main flexion lines are united, signifying emotional instability.*

Occasionally the head line is bridged to the heart line (Figure 45), resembling a simian life line, and indicates that the head controls the heart, or reason overcomes emotion.

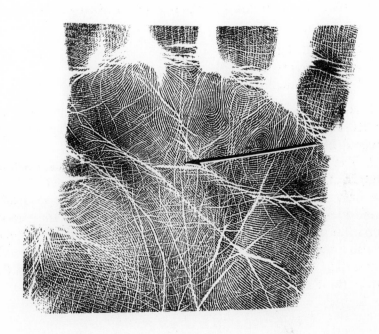

Figure 45. *The heart line and head line in this hand are bridged.*

That brings us to a very important point, namely, one cannot study the head line without considering the heart line — the "signature" of emotion — and we shall deal with this vital line in a separate chapter.

Now I would like to refer you again to Dr. King's statement mentioned at the beginning of this chapter, "... we must be able to read the signature."

Interpretation of Signatures

To understand the mystery of the human mind and emotion one has to develop a talent for interpreting the markings found in the human hand.

The signs in the hand not only tell you something about the nature of your fellowman but they also indicate whether or not you are able to interpret hand signs correctly.

To know thyself and thy fellowman one must have at least one of the following four chiroglyphics which is discussed below:

1. Good head line
2. Medical stigmata
3. Mystic cross
4. Line of intuition or hypothenar line

1. A good head line indicates logic and reasoning and the ability to interpret and analyze findings. This we have already covered in previous pages.

2. The medical stigmata (Figures 46-a and 46-b) is a symbol composed of several short, vertical lines located immediately on the base of the little finger. These signs are almost invariably found in a doctor's palm. They are sometimes called the (good) Samaritan lines, which is self-explanatory. The medical stigmata is also found in the palms of many professional people who spend their lives helping others, such as the members of the Red Cross, the Salvation Army, and hospital personnel.

Figure 46-a. *Medical stigmata, palm print of physician.*

I have observed that very often those who have the medical stigmata exhibit a sympathetic attitude toward the physical needs of others and those without it show the trait of sanguiphobia — fear of the sight of blood.

3. The mystic cross (Figure 47, page 100) is usually found between the heart line and the head line. It indicates an interest in mysticism, the occult, or the esoteric. Unlike crease lines, both the medical stigmata and the mystic cross are not formed by flexion (movement) of the hand. They are signs which nature, unaided by flexion, has placed in some human palms.

4. The line of intuition or the hypothenar line is so named because it encircles the hypothenar eminence, the Mount of Luna (Figure 48).

The line of intuition is often found in a hand which has many atavistic features, indicating that the animal and primitive man have instinct or intuition. It is found in a primitive or elementary hand and could be considered a stigma of degeneration; however, in a well-developed hand it is a sign of extrasensory perception.

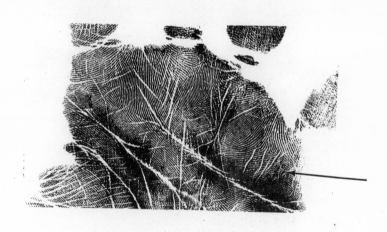

Figure 46-b. *Medical stigmata, palm print of a nurse.*

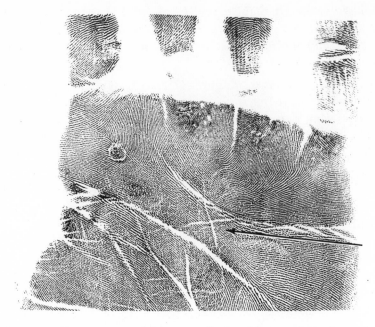

Figure 47. *"Mystic cross," between the head line and the heart line.*

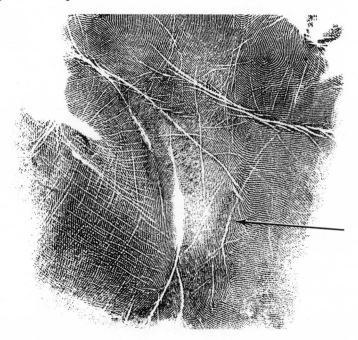

Figure 48. *Line of intuition.*

11

Interpreting the Shape
of the Fingers

The most important tool in studying human nature and health is physiognomy, the interpretation of the shape of the fingers and the muscular development of the latter at their base, known as the mounts.

The difference between the signature of the palm and the shape of the fingers is that the crease line pattern and dermatoglyphics are determined by the inherited genes before birth, and the majority of the configurations of the fingers are caused by hormones after birth.

As stated before, the inherited characteristic in many instances could be modified or even altered by environment or early life experiences. In adverse environmental conditions or during long periods of stress, the endocrine glands could function abnormally and, to a considerable degree, influence the shape and length of the fingers and the muscle of the hand, as well as cause abnormal personality traits.

Therefore, we could assume that crease line patterns are the signs of our inherited characteristics, and physiognomy of the fingers is the mirror of our acquired and modified hereditary behavior patterns.

101

Analysis of the Thumb

We have discussed the diagnostic significance of gestures, postures, and the flexibility of the thumb, but the most distinguishing mark of our personality is the physiognomy of the thumb. Its first phalange section, or the nail phalange, represents willpower and strength of character. The second phalange represents logic and reasoning power.

If the first phalange is short and narrow, it is an indication that the person cannot control his energy because of lack of staying power, indecision, or procrastination.

If you have a strong, long nail phalange but a weak, short second phalange, you like to fulfill your will or desire regardless of whether it is logical or reasonable; in other words, you have a tendency to act without thinking.

Occasionally you find a very short, ill-formed first phalange resembling a clubbed thumb. It is different from the clubbing mentioned previously in relation to heart or lung disorders. It is an indication of inherited, abnormal genes. Unlike the clubbed thumb, the nails are not watch-crystal shaped — they are wide and short.

Because this type of thumb is determined by abnormal genes, we could consider it an atavistic sign — sometimes known as a "murderer's thumb" because some ancient palmist observed it among criminals. But, this name is a misnomer because this type of thumb is frequently found in people with certain endocrine disorders (such as acromegaly or cretinism) and sometimes in normal people.

Nevertheless, we should consider it an unfavorable sign, especially if one finds other abnormal features. As Dr. Charlotte Wolff [1] stated, "It is always a sign of degenerative tendencies, such as some kind of irrational behavior, especially lack of emotional control."

A thumb with a normal length reaches halfway up to the third or bottom phalange of the index finger (Figure 49). A short thumb

---

[1] *The Human Hand,* p. 84.

does not reach to the halfway mark; a long thumb reaches beyond that point (Figure 50 on page 104).

According to all the well-known palmists a long, straight thumb is a true signature of a great man and a strong individual. D'Arpentigny emphasized that great men, humanitarians, and reformers usually have such thumbs; i.e; Danton, Descartes, Newton, and Voltaire.

The majority of famous people I have personally analyzed had long thumbs. The significance of the long thumb is portrayed by Michelangelo in his famous statue of David and his self-portrait.

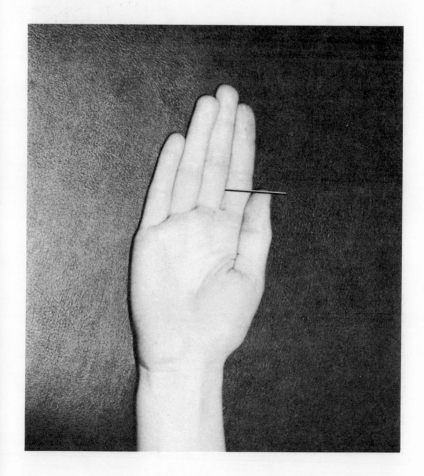

Figure 49. *A thumb of normal length which is indicated by a line.*

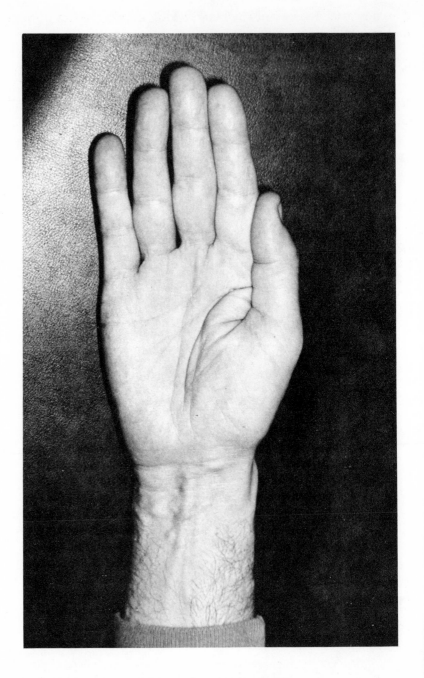

Figure 50. *A long thumb.*

INTERPRETING THE SHAPE OF THE FINGERS

D'Arpentigny, the father of palmistry, concluded that, in want of other proof, the thumb would convince him of the existence of God.

Analysis of the Index Finger

The index finger is sometimes called the "world finger" because it is an indication of the individual's attitude to the external world, his self-assertion, ambition, and aspirations in this world. He uses his finger to order, threaten, and point.

With the gesture of the index finger, man not only tries to exhibit his power to his fellowman but also attempts to reflect his superiority to animals. Dr. Charlotte Wolff stated that the high degree of mobility in the human index finger is incomparable with that of monkeys, who are unable to use this digit separately. And, in addition to its mobility, as she emphasized, the length of the human index finger is another one of its most striking features, because all monkeys have index fingers much shorter than those of man.

In comparing the index finger to the thumb we could state, as Fred Getting (an English palmist) pointed out, that the index finger manifests the world desires and aspirations of the individual. The thumb manifests the amount of energy available to attain those desires. Therefore, if you have a strong index finger and a weak thumb, you will experience difficulties in achieving your life aims.

A well-developed and strong index finger accompanied by a good thumb is an indication of a strong ego structure, which enables a person to adapt himself to any life situation or environment.

The normal index finger reaches the half point of the first phalange of the middle finger and it is about as long or slightly shorter than the fourth or ring finger. If it is longer than the ring finger, it is a sign of an urge for power or dominance. A person with an exceptionally long finger often has a narcissistic complex, is extremely vain, and has a desire to be a leader, ruler, or master. Such people are never content to have a subordinate position in their home, business, profession or social life. They are extremely discriminating, often snobbish, and hard to please.

In contrast, people with abnormally short index fingers have an inferiority complex. They lack pride and ambition, they are dependent, and are willing to be dominated or ruled because they are usually afraid of responsibility and leadership.

An ill-formed, long index finger denotes distorted ego, morbid vanity, or false pride. If it curves to the middle finger, this signifies possessive or acquisitive tendencies.

A well-developed, muscular padding or mount at the base of the index finger emphasizes the significance of the index finger.

The Middle Finger

As the name implies, this finger is in the middle between the conscious and subconscious zone of the hand. It is, as F. Getting pointed out, a sentinel or mediator between the ego or the conscious and the "id" or subconscious aspect. Therefore, we may call it the mirror of our conscience or superego.

If the middle finger is short, undeveloped, and tapered, it is suggestive of an undeveloped superego, or controlling power. These individuals may have a good index finger or even a well-developed thumb, signifying willpower and logic; nevertheless, they will have difficulty in controlling their animalistic or undesirable urges, even though they know that to give in to these urges is wrong. Therefore, we could consider a short middle finger as a sign of irresponsibility.

An exceptionally long middle finger is also an unfavorable sign. It is indicative of emotional conflict. It is often seen in schizophrenic patients and normal people who have a conflict between their emotional and intellectual needs.

Dr. Charlotte Wolff observed that individuals with a long middle finger have a melancholic disposition.

One of the most significant signs is when the middle finger is curved and the first phalange bends toward the ring finger. It is an indication of mental depression. Persons with such a configuration prefer solitude, and if there is no other indication of emotional disturbance but withdrawal or escape from reality, then such a finger should be considered a good sign. People such as these will never be bored or lonely; they like to be alone—to meditate, rest, and listen to soothing music.

The Fourth and Fifth Fingers

As stated before, the thumb and index finger represent the ego or conscious mind; and the middle finger represents the superego or conscience. The ring and the little finger are associated with the "id" or the unconscious. They represent the imaginative and subconscious part of our personality, especially if they are accompanied by a long, strong hypothenar eminence (Mount of Luna).

A person with a well-developed, long ring finger has the capacity to express his imagination or sublimate his unconscious motivation in all forms of art, especially if the mount at the base of the ring finger is large. Even if he is not creative, such a person can enjoy everything that is beautiful or artistic, such as beautiful women, elaborate homes, and elegant or tasteful clothing or dress. He enjoys the beauty of nature, scenic countryside, mountains, valleys, and lakes; therefore, he loves to travel. If he has a strong, straight little finger, he could sublimate his unconscious tension or direct his psychic energy (libido) to a business or profession.

If the index finger is as long as the middle finger, the person will satisfy his subconscious urges or needs by gambling or indulging in pleasure-seeking instincts.

One day, I read the palm of a former Russian aristocrat. He had an exceptionally long ring finger. I told him that he was interested in art, music, and beauty in general, and I concluded that he probably had a beautiful villa, filled with paintings and surrounded with a beautiful garden. He answered that I was right, that he had inherited the villa from his father, but was not crazy about art or music; he preferred gambling. As a matter of fact, he told me that he sold one of his valuable paintings to pay off a gambling debt. His interest in beauty was perhaps found in his appreciation of colorful uniforms (he was an officer in the cavalry), ballets, and balls complete with all the pageantry.

The keynote to this man's character is beautifully portrayed by Tolstoy in his book *War and Peace*. The army officers in the book gambled, drank, and wore beautiful uniforms, and they were accompanied by well-dressed, glamorous women.

The little finger, in reference to its variability of physiognomy, is like the thumb; therefore, we could call it the little thumb.

The length of this finger has important medical significance. The normal length of the fifth finger is to the joint between the first and second phalange of the fourth finger. As Dr. Theodore Berry[2] pointed out, "An abnormally short fifth finger or thumb which may occasionally be found among normal people is, however, a physical aberration which carries a high index of suspicion in the probability of mental or behavioral deviations." In addition, the little finger is profoundly associated with one of the greatest instincts—sex. We shall deal with that when we discuss sexual behavior.

The importance of finger length has been well established but the shape of the fingertips is equally important.

If we assume, as we did in the previous chapter, that the shape of the fingertips is determined by the hormones (such as tapering in pituitary disorders), then we must accept the assertion of all palmists that the tips are also indicative of some personality traits.

Accordingly, we believe that square fingertips (Figure 51)

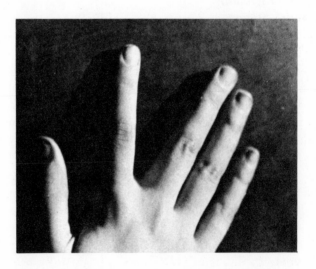

Figure 51. *Square fingers.*

---

[2] *The Hand,* F. A. Davis Co., Philadelphia, Penn., 1963, p. 187.

strengthen our reasoning power, spatulate or spade fingers (Figure 52) increase our activity, and tapering fingers (Figure 53) widen our imagination and our emotion.

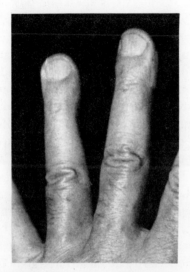

Figure 52. *Spatulate fingers.*

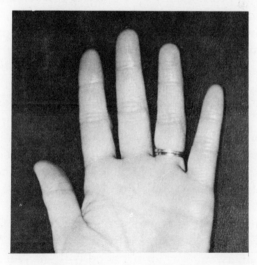

Figure 53. *Conic fingers.*

A person with square fingertips is "square" indeed. He is conventional and a strict observer of social customs. His life is a matter of routine, order, and system. He likes to do the same thing at the same hour each day or at the same day each week. The same is true of his sex life. It is the same day after day, for this is the way he prefers it—same time, same place, same way. The "square" is loyal and this type of person seldom commits adultery.

The spatulate finger is the easiest type to recognize. The broad fingertips resemble the spatula used by the old-time apothecary in a mortar. The owner of this hand is energetic and restless. He loves action, excitement, and adventure, and he cannot tolerate monotony and restrictions. All this applies equally to his sexuality. Always seeking variety and new experiences, he will participate in all kinds of sexual activities. One "spatulate" woman expressed herself, in this way "We like parties with two or more couples with all the stops pulled out."

An individual with tapering or conic fingers tends to be impulsive, impatient, and sensitive, and easily bored by routine. He does not live according to the clock. He eats when he is hungry—and not necessarily at mealtime—goes to bed when he is sleepy, and makes love when he is in the mood.

His sex life has sentimental and romantic overtones and he will enjoy sex to the fullest only if the act is surrounded by mood-producing stimuli. He is easily influenced; therefore, he is fickle. He is intuitive, a dreamer, idealistic, and often impractical. He is impressionable and moody, and what is important to remember, he responds to harmony, beauty, and artistic surroundings.

In conclusion, I should like to advise my readers that to evaluate all the previously mentioned signs of the palm and fingers, one must recognize whether the whole hand is abnormal, average, or normal and whether the hand is a perfect one. This advice is borne out by the point that the abnormal hand intensifies all the aberrations of the palm and fingers while the perfect hand nullifies them.

This classification of the hand symbolizes the fact that in every man there are animal, human, and divine elements. The majority of men have an average or normal hand with many imperfections, denoting that man is not perfect. Very often he acts like an animal, and by trial and error and proper training or education will learn how to control his hostile and animalistic nature.

The perfect hand is a symbol of the sublime evolution of man and his identification with his maker. In the perfect hand we usually find four well-developed lines which form a character resembling the initial "M." Picasso's hand is a good example (Figure 54). The ancient palmists believed that if an individual possessed the symbol M in both hands then he was like God and could master his own destiny, but he must remember that MM signified he was mortal—memento mori, remember death. As a mortal he could be wrong many times (or make mistakes); that is the reason why even a perfect hand has some irregularities.

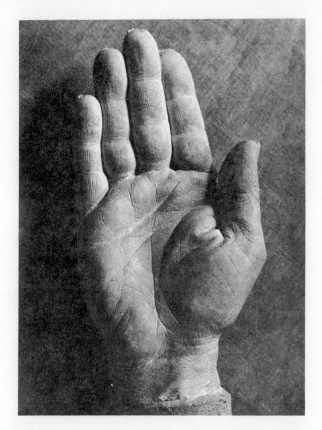

Figure 54. *Plaster cast of Picasso's hand. From* Picasso and Company *by Brassai. Copyright © 1966 by Doubleday & Company, Inc. Reprinted by permission of the author and the publisher.*

In contrast to the perfect hand, there is the abnormal hand which resembles the hand of the primates, indicating an atavistic regression of the individual who must be guided or trained continuously because he very often does the wrong thing.

12

How to Recognize the Beast in Our Midst

Two young men terrorize and murder an entire family in Kansas. . .a student in Texas takes deadly aim from a campus tower and murders 13 innocent people at random. . . eight student nurses are massacred by a drunken ex-sailor in Chicago. . .and more and more senseless crimes of fantastic enormity scream at us from the headlines of our daily newspapers. Ordinary people are horrified when they read of these blood-curdling crimes but never connect events such as these with their own lives. In every small or large community in the world, but especially in America, ordinary, law-abiding citizens go about their affairs completely ignorant of the "beast in their midst"; i.e., that individual who without warning or reason may commit an atrocious crime . . . kill because he must. He is the psychopath . . . usually unknown until he suddenly runs amok and destroys everything and anyone who happens to be near him at the time. What makes him a psychopath? No one knows for sure, but psychiatrists believe that the essential component is present at birth—that factor in his mental makeup which predisposes him toward extreme hostility and abnormal behavior.

113

This component is believed to occur when something interferes with the normal development of the fetus phylogenetically. This means that normally the development of the fetus involves a mental progression from primordial to *homo sapiens*. If the progression is retarded or interfered with, the individual will retain certain atavistic tendencies that are characteristic of our primordial ancestors—our animalistic ancestors.

Psychiatrists recognize symptoms of the psychopathic personality in children at an early age and believe that this abnormality is inherited. Dr. Lauretta Bender, noted child psychiatrist, emphasized that the psychopathic component is present from birth but that symptoms seldom appear before adolescence; therefore, she suggests that a routine psychiatric examination of all school children could reveal indications of psychopathic personality as well as evidence of other emotional disorders.

I believe, as do many students of the human hand, that routine examinations of the palm print of school children could help the psychiatrist recognize tendencies toward a psychopathic personality.

Since it is an established fact that hand prints can give clues to congenital and neurological disorders and mental retardation or disorder, there is no reason to dispute the assumption of a modern palmist that the hand could reveal a potentially psychopathic personality, sexual psychopath, or an individual harboring other latent criminal tendencies.

In my article in the *Psychoanalytic Review* in 1951, I presented a palm print of a sexual psychopath. All the features which indicated his abnormal behavior were present at infancy and before his birth, long before he showed symptoms of abnormal sexual behavior. In some sex criminals, such as the alleged killer of the eight nurses, identification was aided by a fingerprint. I am convinced that the hand could reveal a tendency to kill, long before the crime is committed. The hands of the majority of criminals have abnormal features usually resembling those found on the hand of a monkey.

The abnormal hand features of many psychopaths or criminals indicate that the individual regressed along the path of evolution, because something interfered during the period of fetal growth. It has long been believed by many well-known scientists (such as Haeckel, Blauler, and Freud) that during our fetal growth we recapitulate the mental and bodily evolution of mankind from primordial man to modern man.

How to Recognize Animalistic Signs

To recognize the beast in our midst we should evaluate three important animalistic or atavistic signs: simian line, lack of longitudinal line, and short, deformed thumb. Each is discussed in turn below.

The Simian Line

The genesis of modern palmistry goes back to the year 1909 when Dr. Landon Down discovered that mongolian idiots have a short hand, bearing a single transverse palmar flexion crease, usually found in monkeys—hence the name simian line. Since then, many scientists have investigated this line and observed that it may be found with other abnormalities, as well as with average people. In 1924, Crookshank, in a book entitled *The Mongol in Our Midst*, postulated that a European could acquire some of the features of the Mongolian race by means of regression along the path of human evolution. He had seen a similar crease on the hand of several Chinese sailors, and in the British Museum he saw an 8th-century statue of Buddha whose uplifted hand showed the same configuration. Although he admitted that the single crease was "not generally found in the mixed or higher Mongolian races," he concluded that it was a Mongolian characteristic.

I observed that the simian line is a sign of degeneracy only if accompanied by other atavistic features. It must be emphasized that the simian line in mongolism is always associated with a short thumb, curved little finger, and abnormal palm print patterns, such as a wide-angle axial triradius.

W. Benham, noted American palmist, stated that a subject with a simian line will lose control and often commit crimes when his emotions, feelings, and desires are aroused, and concluded that such a person is not necessarily a criminal. But, if the hand

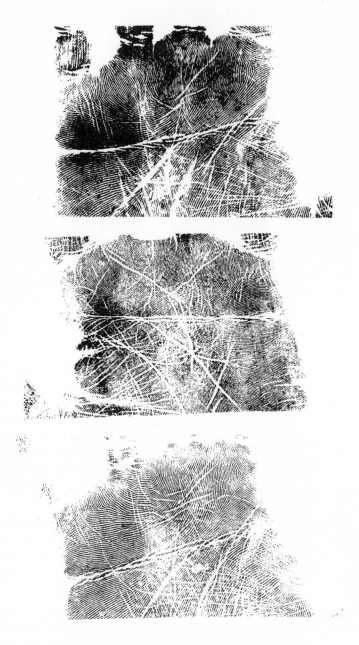

Figure 55. *Examples of simian lines.*

is brutal, the Mount of Venus large, full, and red, nails short, and Mount of Mars large, he will be a criminal who may commit murder to satisfy his desires. He is not strong enough to control the passions which rage within him.

Fred Getting, contemporary London palmist, formed the same opinion substantiating Benham's point when he noted that the simian line occurs in a high proportion of criminal types. The significance of this may lie in the fact that the "normal" personality manages to find a balance between his instincts, emotions, and intellect with a reasonable degree of success. His first impulse is usually different from his final action. He may feel like killing the person who is provoking him, but he will reason himself out of the fatal reaction before his instincts get the better of him. Examples of simian lines are shown in Figure 55.

It is interesting to note that there is a close relation between the palmist's interpretation of the simian line and the psychiatrist's description of the psychopathic personality. According to the palmist, the simian line denotes extremism and single-mindedness. Persons with such a line have tremendous tenacity or intensity of character, for good or evil.

Characteristic of those individuals with a simian line is the equal intensity with which they love or hate. In addition they are extremely egocentric, generally very "wrapped up" in what they want to the exclusion of everything and everybody. Similarly egocentricity is most characteristic of the psychopath. To quote Drs. W. Overholser and W. Richmond, noted psychiatrists, "The world exists for him alone, and anything that interferes with his enjoyment of it or his designs upon it is pushed ruthlessly out of the way. He has feelings enough and his emotions are often violent and unstable, but his feelings are always concerned with himself."

The simian line also signifies a great power of concentration. If there are other unfavorable signs in the hand, the person uses his mental strength to achieve his selfish purpose so cleverly that few will suspect his diabolic aims, and he usually will succeed in avoiding trouble with the law. However, despite his shrewdness, such a person sometimes acts like an emotionally immature child.

Therefore, many palmists also call this line an indication of extremism in behavior. In other words, persons with a simian line could sometimes act like a genius or an idiot. The same applies to many psychopaths, or as Drs. Overholser and Richmond[1] stated, "He may be intelligent, up to the point of genius, or he may be unintelligent, down to mental deficiency . . . The single-mindedness with which the genius often pursues his course, sacrificing everything—wife, family and friends—to his work, caring for nothing except what he has set out to do, certainly recalls the self- centeredness of the psychopath."

The simian line has many forms denoting different mental and emotional attitudes of an individual, and so there are many varieties of the psychopathic personality.

The typical simian line is one straight, lower transverse flexion crease across the palm from side to side. In other words, one strong head line. If, however, the line of the heart is found at the same time, it modifies the qualities of the simian line—indicating these persons, despite their egocentricity, could act as normal human beings, especially if they are not rejected by their parents, their family and friends, and society. The same could be said about some psychopathic personalities—not all are incurable as many psychiatrists assume.

Dr. John M. MacDonald, professor at the University of Colorado, believes that emphasis on the abnormal aspects of the psychopath's character contributes to diagnostic error and should be counterbalanced by greater reference to positive features and possible capacity for mature behavior. The human personality, both normal and abnormal, is full of paradox. For example, he points out that the obsessional character is stubborn, orderly, and miserly but is sometimes compliant, untidy, and generous. We see similar contrasts in the psychopath. Not every situation will evoke the same response. In one instance he may be unreliable, in the next responsible.

Lack of Longitudinal Line

The second abnormal feature of the palm is absence of a longi-

---

[1] Drs. W. Overholser and W. Richmond, *Handbook of Psychiatry*, J. B. Lippincott, 1947.

tudinal line (Figure 56) due to the lack of longitudinal flexibility of the hand. This line is sometimes called the line of opposition, and in normal hands usually begins in the wrist and runs upward toward the base of the index finger. The simian line is a result of a simian characteristic trait, namely grasping. The line of opposition is determined by a distinctive human trait, namely the opposition movement of the thumb. The simian line is formed in intrauterine life, representing inherited genes or chromosomal, congenital, or constitutional defects. Therefore, we associate the simian line with our constitution—part of our inheritance—what we bring at birth. In contrast, the line of opposition is absent at birth and usually develops during our early childhood; its length and characteristics are determined by the environmental experiences in our childhood. That is why the palmist calls this important line the fate line.

A long, well-developed fate line indicates that the individual has the necessary inner strength to control his own fate. I like to call this crease the line of maturity because a man with such a line has adaptability, determination, and perseverance; he has the ability to face reality and cope with it. A man with an undeveloped fate line is emotionally immature, listless, and weak and, like a child or an animal, he is depending entirely on environmental forces, becoming, at times, a victim of them. He lacks purpose in life and has no sense of direction, no determination, and an undeveloped superego. This is why the majority of criminals and mental defectives have no fate line. Dr. Charlotte Wolff calls the fate line the line of superego because it is the mirror of our conscience. She observed that the hands in which the long longitudinal line is lacking are abnormal hands and are usually accompanied by the simian line. In her study of 532 mental defectives, Dr. Wolff found that in 224 cases there was no fate line and in 50 cases the simian line was present. In another study of 45 delinquent French boys at a Paris clinic, she noticed that the fate line in the hands of 20 was completely lacking; in *the remainder it was imperfectly developed.*

It would seem that the lack of a fate line is more significant than the presence of a simian line, especially in diagnosing a psychopath. The lack of or a faulty fate line signifies the absence or faulty development of the superego or the conscience—a critical

Figure 56. *Palm prints without fate lines.*

factor in cases of psychopathic personality. As Dr. R. S. Banay,[2] Chief of Staff, Civic Center Clinic for Rehabilitation of Offenders, Brooklyn, New York, expressed it, ". . . lack of, or deficiency in, conscience appears to account for the psychopath's obliviousness to ethical standards. With faint or faulty conscience, he simply seems to have failed to acquire those moral controls that keep most people within the acceptable social standard."

The Short, Deformed Thumb

However important the simian line and the lack of fate line may be, they are not conclusive unless they are accompanied by the most important atavistic sign — a short, stiff, and deformed thumb. It is this phenomenon which is occurring in a much higher percentage of abnormal people than either of the two other characteristics. It is the straight, long thumb which really differentiates us from the primates and it is the crucial sign in recognizing the beast in our midst. A short, undeveloped thumb, as stated before, is a sign of lack of logic or reason and also is an indication of the inability to learn. This is very characteristic of the psychopath because he is unable to learn from experience.

Although the previously mentioned atavistic features are indications of abnormal personality, I must warn you not to jump to conclusions if you discover two or three of these signs in your own or another person's hand, because these features only show a predisposition to abnormal behavior and *not* necessarily the presence of a personality disorder.

I have met many people with a simian line and deformed thumb who were perfectly adjusted and normal individuals because they had happy and well-adjusted childhoods. On the other hand, I know people whose behavior exhibits emotional instability, egocentricity, antisociality, and rebellious activities despite the fact that their hands do not show any signs of degeneracy.

---

[2] "Psychopath or Sociopath," *The Encyclopedia of Mental Health*, Albert Deutsch, Editor, Vol. 5, N.Y., 1963.

Analysis Dependent on Whole Hand

To analyze the main atavistic features, we must consider the hand as a whole and learn to interpret other signs on the hand.

The following hand features will intensify the significance of the three crucial atavistic signs:

1. Highly placed axial triradius,
2. Excess whorls on the finger, usually more than six, and on the Mount of Venus or Mount of Luna,
3. Unusually red, stiff, and habitually cold hands,
4. Coarse texture of the skin.

Besides these supporting clues, handwriting can also provide some important evidence because it often reveals abnormal personality traits.

But, the most important factor in diagnosing a psychopathic personality is his early home environment, especially his relation to his mother. It should be noted that, as the atavistic signs indicate, he has an animalistic nature; but, like the majority of animals, he could be tamed and the best qualified trainer is his mother (or a mother substitute). The following case history is a good example of the significance of the mother in relation to the fate of a child who is born with animalistic components.

Case History of Fate of a Child Born with Animalistic Components

This concerns a male, age 38 at the time of this writing. He was born into a well-to-do family who provided him everything necessary for the normal development of a child: good home, medical care, nursing, education, entertainment, and, above all, love and attention from a mother. Consequently, he had a satisfactory adjustment to life during his first two decades. He behaved normally and was a model child and student. As he stated, "I never did anything wrong; never lied, cursed, or insulted anyone. And, believe it or not, I never masturbated or had any sexual relations until I got married."

He graduated with good marks and became a teacher. He was

liked by his pupils, colleagues, and principal because he was dedi-
cated to his profession. For two years he had a satisfactory marital
life and had one child. However, he proved to be oversexed. Later,
his wife became resentful because, as she stated, she "couldn't
stand it any longer." However, he insisted and when she was un-
cooperative he acted like a "cave man" and became so brutal that
she left him. After the divorce he developed a hostility toward
every woman and soon became involved in homosexual relations.
He became emotionally unstable and gave up his profession because he was "too nervous to teach."

He moved to Chicago where he bought a shop because he
wanted to please one of his "lovers" who was in the same line of
business. He learned the trade and started a new phase of his life.
He appeared to be contented because he was able to satisfy his
pleasures — food, sex, and work in his shop. After six years he
underwent another crisis: he had to sell his shop, taking a loss,
because of urban renewal, and could not find another suitable
location except in another part of town. His boyfriend refused
to go with him, and broke up the relationship. After this he developed hostility toward everyone. He became disturbed and tried
to escape for a period of time in drinking. He met another man
he liked and, after he inherited some money, bought an apartment building which he and his boyfriend managed.

After four years they are still together. His friend is loyal to
him and does everything to please him. One day I explained to
this new associate that as long as he shows kindness he will be
rewarded because his friend loves him with intensity and advised
him not to hurt him because his love could turn to hate. "Don't
worry, Doc," he replied to me, "I won't hurt Santa Claus, he
willed his apartment to me." He concluded, "I wish I could make
him happier. He's not a happy man. Can't sleep and can't smile,
all he is interested in is working and drinking."

The patient's palm shows a typical imprint of a "beast" (or
animal nature). Short thumb and short little finger, simian line,
faulty fate line, and other abnormal chiroglyphics. Also, another
significant atavistic feature he exhibits is that his palm is longer
than his fingers. Despite these congenital aberrations of the hand
he is not a criminal, nor is he destructive. His symptoms point
to a psychoneurotic pattern rather than to a psychopathic person-

ality. The reason for this, I believe, is because in his early childhood he was tamed and conditioned by his parents.

The majority of congenital psychopaths, however, do not have satisfactory childhood influences because chances are they inherited some abnormal traits from their parents. In such cases, one could detect some abnormal or antisocial behavior pattern in childhood.

Therefore, if an adolescent or a child shows extreme stubbornness, lack of discipline, and egocentric behavior and his hand has a majority of the atavistic and other abnormalities described here, you may suspect that he may have a psychopathic personality.

I should like to emphasize that you can only *suspect* and not diagnose a psychopath. Even psychiatrists have difficulty in recognizing such abnormal personalities. Because, as Dr. Walter Bromberg pointed out in the *Archives of General Psychiatry*:[3]

> ". . . that the psychopathic personality diagnosis is a wastebasket—too generalized, too inexact, too all-inclusive . . ."

Despite all the difficulties, you could learn a great deal about abnormal behavior through medical palmistry. You could even detect a beast in our midst if you analyze many hands, and learn to recognize the different types of personality found in the normal or average man.

---

[3] "Psychopathic Personality Concept Evaluated and Re-evaluated," December, 1967.

13

The Importance of Personality Types and How to Recognize Them

There are no two temperaments or personalities exactly alike. Each individual will react differently, in some degree, to the same stimulation. Each individual will cope with life differently. Therefore, to understand the environmental reactions and life experiences of a man, we need to classify the basic differences between people.

Many attempts have been made to classify human differences, but no standard formula has yet been worked out which could be applied to the study of mankind. I have analyzed more than 1,000 men of different character and have come to the same conclusion as did many others such as Dr. Eric Berne, author of *Games People Play*, that Dr. W. H. Sheldon, a pioneer in constitutional psychology, and his associates set up the best and most adequate classification of human nature, based on the physique of an individual.

The Three Basic Body Builds

According to Dr. Sheldon, there are three basic body builds which develop from the three embryonic layers, which are the *endoderm, mesoderm,* and *ectoderm.*

The endoderm, the inner layer, grows into our digestive system and other inner organs of our abdomen. The mesoderm, the middle layer, gives rise to our body structure — the bone, muscle, and connective tissue. The ectoderm, the outside layer, provides our skin, brain, and nervous system.

Generally these layers grow equally; therefore, the average person has equal amounts of these components. In some cases, however, one layer grows more than the other two and will influence the character of the body build and the behavior of an individual to a certain degree.

Individuals with an overdeveloped digestive system will have a large stomach, large abdomen, broad hips, and big buttocks. They will be fat with well-rounded faces. These people are called endomorphs.

If the middle layer, the mesoderm, is overgrown, we speak of a mesomorphic body build which is characterized by having well-developed muscles, strong bones, and a well-developed heart. If the outside layer is the predominant one, the person will have a thin, long, fragile body usually with a flat chest and poor posture. He is called an ectomorph.

Each of these body types has distinctive personality traits which can easily be explained by the words of Dr. Eric Berne: The endomorph is "digestive-minded," the mesomorph is "muscle-minded," and the ectomorph is "brain-minded." The scientific names of these temperaments are respectively, viscerotonia, somatotonia, and cerebrotonia and will be discussed later in this chapter.

To emphasize the importance of the interrelation of body build and personality, I would like to quote the directors of the famous Gesell Institute of Child Behavior — Drs. Frances L. Ilg[1] and

---

[1] *The Gesell Institute's Child Behavior*, Perennial Library, Harper & Row, Publisher, New York, 1966, p. 43.

Louise B. Ames.[1] They observed many children and came to the following conclusion: "The study of personality assessment based on measurement of bodily structure actually covers every aspect of human behavior. From the way a human being is built, many scientists believe they can predict how he might act — his eating, sleeping, social behavior, what kinds of situations he will seek or avoid, the possibility or impossibility of his being a success in activities requiring physical skill."

Dr. Arnold Gesell, the founder of this institution, expressed this more significantly. He stated, "In the shape of his physique the newborn infant already gives token of what he is to be. He has constitutional traits and tendencies, largely inborn, which determine how, when, to some extent even what he will learn."

Relation of Palmistry to Physique Analysis

Despite the importance of constitutional psychology, many observers believe that as long as the classification of human types is limited to the physique only, it will remain of questionable value because there are very few pure human types. However, if we associate the study of body physique with the study of the shape of the hand (physiognomy), we will be able to distinguish a greater number of pure types, especially if we implement the study with an analysis of the subjects' handwriting. It is very important to keep in mind that, whatever importance the physique has in relation to personality, it becomes insignificant if we ignore the study of the human hand — the most mobile, sensitive, and expressive part of our constitution. A study of the hand and handwriting will enable us to divide Dr. Sheldon's threefold classification division into sharper and clearer psychological types and could make constitutional psychology more applicable to understanding human differences.

In this chapter, we shall subdivide the three body types into nine classes. If you familiarize yourself with the differences in the structure of the human hand, you will be able to understand differences in human behavior. In our classifications, we shall use a simple and descriptive terminology. (The terms used by the constitutional psychologist are confusing.)

Before we divide this threefold system, we must emphasize

that the features of the constitution, hand, or handwriting do not matter. *It is the description of the temperament we are concerned with.* Certain psychological types exist and we must recognize them to know ourselves and our fellowmen.

Although basically the classifications of body type and personality apply to both men and women, this discussion of personality is mainly about men. Women are a mystery. As a rule, palmists do not make the generalizations about women that it is possible to make about men. A woman's makeup and problems are more complex than a man's. She is basically a mother and her instincts in the home or a career are those of a mother. The majority of women do not project their personality in marriage and they learn to sublimate — in other words, their family comes first. Many college girls leave school after a year or two to get married and start a home. Even the single, career women — in spite of what they may say — want to get married and will give up their careers for marriage and a home when they have the opportunity to do so.

The Fixed Type
Viscerotonia (Key word — Rigidity)

The physique for this type as a whole is characterized by a large, round, stocky body, a wide face and a short neck, broad cheeks and a big abdomen, small bones, and short limbs. The hand is stiff and often contracted and so is the handwriting. The fingers are shorter than the palm.

The general style of writing is fixed — at times cramped — usually it is old-fashioned with little or no originality. Letters are contracted and carefully drawn with slowness, excessive pressure, and deliberate regularity.

F.1 **The Elementary Type**

He is good-natured, quiet, and simple. His reactions are slow and as a rule he is not sensitive. But his jealousy or other primitive passions are easily aroused and he is inclined to become violent. His mentality is undeveloped. He is not imaginative or sentimental, but he has good memory and intuition. His expressive movements are coarse and brutal. He lives a primitive life which consists mostly of sleeping, drinking, and eating. Strong family attraction, love of company, and indifference to pain is also characteristic of this type.

MARRIAGE AND VOCATION: He is a good father and a loyal husband, but a poor lover because he is interested only in his own sexual instinct. His wife is a slave. Unskilled labor and farm work is best suited for him.

HAND AND HANDWRITING: The fingers are short in relation to the palm, indicating his atavistic nature. The thumb is short. He has a strongly developed thenar eminence or Mount of Venus which makes the thenar or life line long and deep, signifying his strong constitution. The hand is large and muscular with a hard, thickened skin. The palm has very few lines, which characterize lack of sensitivity. His handwriting is heavy, coarse, and elementary.

F.2 The Dominating Type

He is pleasant, cheerful, friendly, and his manner and appearance radiate joy of life when in congenial surroundings. He has great pride, self-reliance, complacency, and often such a degree of self-centeredness that he becomes conceited, vain, and prone to show off. When he talks, he expects absolute silence, and when he acts he wants to be watched and applauded. His fondness of affection is an unconscious desire to inflate his ego, for he likes the spotlight. He wants to be glorified, flattered, and honored. Essentially, he is conservative, but human and tolerant. He has an atavistic nature, strong instinct, robust constitution, and desires to be a "lion," the king of all animals. When his feelings are injured, he flies into a temper and insults his associates, but repents later, for he is too loyal not to be reconciled again. Kindness is his best quality, but he can be a tyrant.

SEX AND MARRIAGE: Great pride characterizes his love, and his ideals are often high. He wants to be proud of his wife; hence, she should always be well dressed and must act like a lady. She must also be a good housekeeper, for he demands neatness and order. All is well as long as he is king in his home and his mate is the queen, subordinated to him. He wants all the attention and flattery, which he feels he deserves. Marriage is sacred to him, and only a serious cause can break up his home.

VOCATION: He prefers a profession that requires executive ability and handling people; hence, a position of authority is best suited for him because he doesn't like to take orders from others. Precision work doesn't appeal to him because he is always interested in big things. He can be a good promoter, financier, bridge-builder, architect, director, or executive in big business.

HAND AND HANDWRITING: The hand is broad and fleshy, its fingers are stout and have a rounded tip. The Mount of Venus and the pads beneath the fingers are strongly developed. His gestures are heavy and slow; therefore the flexion lines appear to be deep and wide and are few in number. The head line and the life line are separated. The thumb is not flexible and his writing is large and rounded and usually ornate; i.e., the capitals and the beginning strokes are flourished. He applies strong writing pressure and uses heavy, descending strokes with long, fat loops. The capitals, especially the pronoun I, are high and conspicuously larger than the smaller letters. Words are close together.

F.3 The Realistic Type

He is practical, conservative, and a slow thinker, who likes to contemplate and meditate, in contrast to F.2 who often acts on impulse. He also has great body strength. His instincts are powerful and often right. Perhaps that is the reason he likes to have his own way and is so hard to convince in an argument. His behavior is relaxed, unhurried, easygoing, friendly, and calm. Trivial things never bother him; but, when he is aroused, he becomes furious. He is self-centered, dogmatic, determined, persistent, and very bullheaded; nevertheless, he has a good sense of humor and is very dependable. In spite of his magnetic personality and his insatiable longing for company, he has few friends because he is selective and very unfriendly if surrounded by people who are not congenial. He is not athletically inclined and at times he is lazy.

SEX AND MARRIAGE: He is a considerate, courteous, and constant lover. Although he is not demonstrative in his affections or sentimental, he will sacrifice and do everything in the world for the one he loves. He will buy some extravagant gift to show that he is devotedly in love. Sex is more or less a habit with him. His wife must furnish him with an easy chair, for he loves comfort. She must be a good cook, but she must not serve him too much sweet or rich food because he loves them and may become too fat. Fancy cooking or canned goods do not appeal to him. He likes food as his mother used to prepare it. His home life must be according to a strict schedule, and everything should run smoothly. He wants to appear dignified; hence, his wife should never play jokes on him. Patience is a virtue, and it is important that his wife learn to be patient, for it is often difficult to put up with him. However, he can be a wonderful husband.

VOCATION: In many respects, it is the same as F.2, but he prefers work which is based on routine and doesn't require too much imagination.

HAND AND HANDWRITING: The hand manifestations are similar to F.2, except the head and the life line are closely attached. The shape of the palm and the fingers are square or rectangular. The muscular pattern is firmer and the index finger is not as long. His most revealing hand characteristic is a very stiff thumb. In writing, the capitals are not large but they are simple and graceful. The punctuation and every letter are carefully made. The style is neat, rounded, and somewhat shaded. The descending loops are well developed, signifying his realistic nature and the ascending loops are not high. The words are connected and often end with a hook or in strokes instead of loops.

The Dynamic Type
Somatotonia (Key word—Activity)

The physique for this type as a whole is characterized by a strong-boned, heavily muscled body, a thick, strong face, a wide neck, and broad shoulders. The hand is muscular and the fingers and palm are about equal in size. The handwriting is energetic, speedy, and angular.

D.1   **The Impulsive Type**

He possesses an aggressive martial energy. He has an insatiable longing for physical adventure, excitement, noise, and the zest of competition. He craves for leadership and has an instinctive urge to be first in everything; hence, he often appears to be selfish. This temperament is not an offensive egotism but an expression of dynamic energy which enables him to wage a good fight, to pioneer into new ventures, and blaze new trails. This energy, if properly controlled or sublimated, could be beneficial to his fellowmen; if not, it is very destructive. His love of sports and athletics often helps him to sublimate his aggressiveness, especially in his youth. He is the type who runs away from home because he cannot stand restriction.

He is courageous, self-assertive, and independent. He often has the first and last word in an argument. His optimism leads him to undertake greater tasks than he can master. Impatience, and his impetuosity are his worst qualities. Slow-moving people irritate him because he is always in a hurry. He makes friends easily, but his friendships do not last long because of his arrogance, conceit, and quarrelsome disposition.

In many instances this temperament is controlled by his parents during his early childhood; but, in later life during mental and physical strain this repressed urge reappears. The reappearance of this repressed temperament happened very often during war stress; but, unfortunately, it was not recognized by many psychiatrists. They failed to realize that the most important criterion in treatment of a psychoneurotic of this type is "need of action when troubled" and not the rest treatment most of them received as part of their psychotherapy.

SEX AND MARRIAGE: He believes in action when it comes to love and will do everything to win the affection of a girl who is hard to get. In college he will go out with the most popular girl and when he conquers her, he will look for new adventure. He is possessive and consequently jealous.

His positive nature will drive him to be superior to his wife, but he wants to be proud of his wife also. His wife must be exciting and interesting and she must give him mental and spiritual inspiration. She must know all the tricks in sex and always be ready to satisfy him without the preliminaries of lovemaking. There is never a dull moment in his marriage, if it lasts.

VOCATION: He is interested in work requiring physical strength, travel, and plenty of activity — no close confinement or routine job for him.

HAND AND HANDWRITING: The life line and the head line are widely separated (courage, impetuosity, and self-reliance) and the index finger is long, often longer than the ring finger. The joints are not as rigid as the fixed type. There is a well-developed muscular pattern on the palm (especially at the base of the index finger) and the thumb, but there is more firmness in the muscle than in the fixed hand as well as more lines.

The writing is angular and energetic with a heavy pressure and firm strokes. The letters are usually large, hurriedly written, and often disconnected. Capitals, especially the "I," are high. The lower loops are long and the letters "a" and "o" are open at the top. The slope is forward.

D.2 The Practical Type

His energy is directed in practical and useful lines. He is industrious, deliberate, and forceful, but cautious, while D.1 is more for adventure and competition. His goal must be more or less assured. His best qualities are his love of work and his ambition. His weak spots are love of attainment, lack of patience, and intolerance of opposition. He is outspoken, independent, egotistical, and somewhat ruthless. He attaches importance to convention and custom. He usually is not very generous and he is not easy to deal with.

SEX AND MARRIAGE: His sexual urge is strong but well controlled. He is a devoted and loyal lover, and, if necessary, he will fight for his loved one. If a girl likes to sleep late in the morning, she should never marry this type for he likes to arise early and he will not tolerate a lazy wife. He likes to run his hours on a strict schedule. His wife must be a good housekeeper and a good cook since he doesn't like going to a restaurant. Although he is sometimes deceitful, he detests lies.

VOCATION: He is especially fitted for a job requiring physical stamina, hard work, organizing power, constructive ability, and accuracy. He is an excellent manager and a good worker if there is a profit in it.

HAND AND HANDWRITING: His hand features are similar to the hand of F.3, but the fingers are longer and not as stiff. The palm contains more lines. Its muscular pattern is firmer.

His writing is small, energetic, and angular but it displays more regularity than D.1. Punctuation and T crossbars are carefully executed. The descending loops are strongly developed and the letters are close together and connected. Little or no margin is characteristic of his writing. The slope is usually vertical or to the left. His signature is strong and often underscored.

The Mutable Type—Cerebrotonia
(Key word—Flexibility)

The physique for this type as a whole is characterized by a thin, slender body, a narrow face, a long, thin neck, and a flat chest. The hand is long and thin with flexible fingers and mobile joints— a delicate hand — and there is a lack of muscular development. The fingers are longer than the palm. There is wide space between the head line and the heart line. The accessary lines are abundant. The handwriting indicates speed and flexibility, which is characterized by the amplification of letter contours and wide, loose writing.

M.1   The Changeable Type

He has a sensitive and excitable nature which is constantly swayed by environment and the mood of other people. His emotions are quickly aroused, but his endurance is not strong. He is idealistic, studious, and fond of all mental recreation and educational pursuits, such as reading or experimenting.

He is curious, but very skeptical. At times he is restless, tense, and nervous, but in emergencies he acts calmly. He is flighty and superficial and changes his mind frequently. For example, one day he wants to travel, the next day he wants to stay home; one minute he is happy, the next minute he is sad.

Mentally he is timid and often cannot make up his mind; however, he can be very shrewd and cunning. He prefers to work alone and solves his own problems without the help of others. He usually thinks and acts for himself.

SEX AND MARRIAGE: He is fickle and changeable; hence, his wife will have difficulties with him. Marriage must provide him with lots of amusement and varieties. His wife must be gay, cheerful, and entertaining. A jealous wife will be miserable with him because he loves to flirt. However, their marriage can be successful because he can have two loves at the same time. He can love his secretary and be perfectly happy with his wife.

VOCATION: He is best in work which requires knowledge and creative and inventive ability. He is versatile and naturally gifted for literature, acting, and journalism. He will succeed in any profession which enables him to develop his active brain, imagination, ingenuity, and manual skill.

HAND AND HANDWRITING: He has a very flexible, narrow, and delicate hand. The thumb is often supple-jointed and the fingers can be bent backward. The little finger is long and has a well-developed eminence at its base, but the Mount of Venus is flat. The crease lines are thin and numerous. The head line and life line are separated. The style of writing is changeable, with small letters of uneven height. The pressure is light. The ovals are open, the upper loops are extended, and the capitals and T bar are varied. The slope is generally forward, at times varying.

M.2   The Analytical Type

He possesses a very discriminating nature, analytical intellect, and a restless temperament. In many respects he has the same characteristics as M.1, (i.e., sensitive, talkative, tense, fond of learning, works alone), except he is more cautious and more prudent, but he is also influenced very much by his surroundings and constantly swayed by emotion. He is mentally very active and versatile, and he is often a walking encyclopedia. At times, he is undecided because of lack of self-confidence. Socially he is very shy, worrisome, and nervous. He is somewhat skeptical and very fussy about his surroundings, his clothing, and his food. He is a fault-finder and an eternal critic.

SEX AND MARRIAGE: He is not an ardent or affectionate lover. His emotional control is so rigid that he seldom falls "madly" in love or is tempted by any vice. The urge of purity and his sense of good taste are his emotional censors. He keeps his affection on a mental level, and insists that his love or romance should progress according to a well-organized code of conduct. His perfectionism and old maidish nature bring him many disappointments in his marital life; hence, he is better off if he doesn't get married until middle age when he is more settled. He has plenty of time because he never shows his age and always has a youthful appearance; perhaps, this is hereditary or because of his chaste and healthy life. Diet and cleanliness are his sensitive points; hence, his wife should be a good dietician and a good housekeeper. She must learn to serve nourishing and appetizing meals because of his delicate appetite. She must be neat, orderly, and have plenty of patience, for he is often narrow-minded, fussy, and will criticize everything. He will look under the rug to see whether his wife sweeps the dirt under it.

VOCATION: He is best fitted for brain work or social work. He is accurate, systematic, and thorough in his work; hence, he could be a good statistician, auditor, pharmacist, cashier, etc. He is interested in small details and likes to analyze everything and everyone. Therefore, he could excel in medical and other scientific research.

HAND AND HANDWRITING: The hand is essentially the same as M.1, except that the head line and the life line are closely attached. His palm lacks muscular development; hence, it appears flat and bony. The little finger is usually shorter than that of M.1 and the joints are not as flexible. The handwriting is similar to M.1, except the letters are not disconnected and there is more regularity and legibility. Small writing is the main characteristic.

M.3 **The Sensitive Type**

He is a repressed, solitary, introverted person who is oversensitive and susceptible to emotion. His main characteristics are lack of self-esteem, self-confidence, apprehensiveness, moodiness, exaggeration, and unpredictability of attitude. He is a true idealist and dreamer who likes to gaze at life through rose-colored glasses and build air castles. If things don't go according to his vivid imagination, he becomes melancholic, procrastinating, and self-indulgent.

His impracticability, undependability, carelessness, and lethargy are his common faults. He likes to be alone; nevertheless, he is very sympathetic and loves animals, children, and the underdog. Through his adaptability he makes friends easily. Art, especially music, religion, and mysticism are his refuge.

At times he is inclined to be overanxious and he becomes very easily disillusioned. He is indecisive at times and lacks in life and energy. He needs a backseat driver or someone who inspires him. He is always afraid that something is going to happen. He is intuitive and psychically receptive.

SEX AND MARRIAGE: He is very affectionate and demonstrative, if someone loves him, and needs all the attention his wife or sweetheart can give him. His shyness and timidity may retard him in achieving success in life unless he has a wife who can encourage and push him ahead. She must bolster his inferiority complex by flattering but not by nagging or driving. She must be a diplomat and an actress who knows how to create the necessary background for a sensitive, sentimental, and emotional nature. In sex she must make advances if necessary, and it is important that she learn all the techniques of lovemaking. He must be in the mood and often needs stimulation to arouse his sexual interest.

HAND AND HANDWRITING: The hand appears to be feminine, slender, and flexible, and the muscles are weak. The fingertips are tapering and graceful. The outstanding features of his handwriting are grace, fluency, amplification of letter contours, wide, loose writing, little pressure, and irregularity.

The foregoing classifications deal only with the ideal cases or pure types, and represent only a small minority of mankind. Most people are mixed types.

While the temperament of the pure type is mainly determined by heredity, the temperament of the mixed type is chiefly determined by early environmental conditioning and life experiences. However, among the mixed types, each human being has his own individual personality, which is reflected in his palm and handwriting.

It should be noted that no two palm prints and no handwriting are alike. Each individual's palm print and handwriting is unique. But if you learn to interpret them, learn what questions to ask the subject, and learn to evaluate his answer in relation to your findings, you may be able to understand his personality, regardless of how unique it may be.

What can you do if you recognize certain unfavorable personality traits of your own and your loved ones, especially your child? My answer is that of Drs. Ilg and Ames.[1]

> "First of all, recognize your child's individuality for what it is and give up the notion that you either produce (except through inheritance) or that you basically change it. Recognize it, understand it, accept it.
>
> "Understand your child's basic and inescapable endowments. Help him to understand himself. Then try to provide, so far as you can, the kind of situation in which each kind of child can feel comfortable and can do well. But don't try to change him and make him over."

---

[1] *The Gesell Institute's Child Behavior*, Perennial Library, Harper & Row, Publisher, New York, 1966, pp. 64-65.

III

THE HANDS—A
RECORD OF PSYCHE

14

Diseases of Anxiety Can Be
Traced Through Palmistry

Before the discovery of vaccines, antibiotics, and vitamins, infectious and nutritional diseases constituted the greatest medical problems. Today, medicine faces an equally serious problem in psychosomatic disturbances and diseases which are mentally based. The majority of individuals who consult a physician today suffer from emotional ailments.

Many investigators of recognized reputation conclude that each individual will react differently to the same environmental stress. Some will suffer from nervous breakdown, some will be afflicted by physical diseases (such as diabetes, asthma, or skin disorders), and still others will develop tension headaches, chest pain, or tension backaches. For instance, certain slim, bony ectomorphs may be destined to be more prone to anxiety neurosis and stomach and bowel disorders, while certain muscular or athletic mesomorphs may be more prone to heart disease, and the round and fat endomorph may be prone to gall bladder attack.

The human hand is a key to understanding anxiety and its consequences. It not only reflects our emotional state but also helps us recognize our particular body type and our possible reactions

141

to extreme stress. Since recognizing our body types is an important factor in evaluating psychosomatic disorders, we can use the infinite clues provided by the hand for treatment and prevention of anxiety and anxiety symptoms.

"The hand is one of the outstanding representatives of the emotions," states Dr. Leland E. Hinsie,[1] professor of psychiatry at Columbia University. "We speak of the heavy hand in states of oppression, of the slack hand denoting idleness, of the helping hand of cheerfulness and cooperation, of the light hand of gentleness, of the strict hand of severe discipline, of the strong hand of force, of the hand-in-glove of familiarity, of the hand-over-head of negligence, of the black hand of lurid crime, etc."

Likewise, the first gesture of the infant — the grasping reflex or the grasping of the thumb — signifies his anxiety about his new environment. When he grows up it will be his hand which will express his anxiety, when like an infant he feels insecure.

In this chapter, we will discuss the important aspects of palmistry in reference to certain common diseases associated with anxiety: (1) anxiety neurosis, (2) stomach ulcers, and (3) coronary heart disease. These diseases will be covered in the discussion below.

Anxiety Neurosis

An attack of acute anxiety (feeling of impending doom) is manifested by physical symptoms such as sweating, choking, shortness of breath, palpitations and extreme fatigue. These physical manifestations are accompanied by an oppressive feeling of sadness, hopelessness, and tension. Chronic anxiety is a steady, prolonged disturbance of mood with the same persistent physical manifestations as acute anxiety but it is less intense.

In the study of this common psychological ailment it is important to keep two factors in mind: (1) anxiety neurosis or acute anxiety attack usually occurs in constitutionally predisposed individuals; (2) repeated anxiety attacks may cause some permanent personality disorders. It is essential that we should learn to

---

[1] *Understandable Psychiatry*, The Macmillan Co., New York, 1948, p. 12.

recognize early constitutional tendencies toward anxiety neurosis or anxiety attacks so we may be able to help these individuals before they develop a psychoneurotic personality.

The gesture, the structure of your hand, and your handwriting can help you diagnose both actual or latent predisposition to anxiety neurosis.

A comparison of your palm print with those of your parents could help you find an answer to a pertinent question that Dr. David Henderson,[1] professor emeritus of the University of Edinburgh raised, "How far is the habit of anxiety, which appears to favour the development of anxiety symptoms, based on inherited emotionality; how far a mere infection, as it were, from an anxious parent . . ."

If palm prints of yours and your parents have a similar dermatoglyphic pattern of congenital neurosis, (see Chapter 8) then you could assume that you inherited a predisposition to neurotic types of reaction, especially if your mother had repeated anxiety attacks during your early childhood.

The dermatoglyphic signs of inherited neurotic constitution have diagnostic significance only if they are accompanied by other hand features which develop during early infancy or childhood and signify both inherited and early acquired neurotic tendencies. The following are the most significant signs:

1. *Abundance of Accessory Lines on the Palm* — The palm print of most nervous and sensitive people is usually covered with many fine lines resembling a spider web. Some observers believe that these lines are the direct result of the involuntary gestures and movements of the hand of a restless and nervous person during his early childhood. To quote Dr. Charlotte Wolff,[2] "The more frequent and complex are a person's nervous and emotional stimuli, the more will emotional tension and nervousness be produced in him, and this will affect the scale and variety of his involuntary movements and gestures and will be registered in the accessory crease lines of the palm."

---

[1] *Henderson and Gillespie's Text Book of Psychiatry*, Oxford University Press, London, 1962.
[2] *The Human Hand*, A. A. Knopf Co., New York, 1944, p. 124.

We can safely assume that an abundance of crease lines (Figure 57) indicates a highly strung, receptive, and sensitive person and, in contrast, the absence of accessory crease lines (Figure 58) signifies a calm individual who lacks sensitivity.

2. *Long, Narrow Palm* — A hand with a long, narrow palm, especially if it is extremely flexible and graceful with tapering fingers, long and narrow nails, and a skin texture fine and smooth, is a true mirror of a delicate and nervous constitution. This type of hand is sometimes called "the sensitive or psychic hand." Possessors of such a hand are very sensitive to environmental stress and often get emotionally upset even in relatively normal circumstances. Like children, these people frequently express their emotional instability or anxiety by complaining of symptoms of illness such as pain, shortness of breath, rapid heart beat, "lump in the throat," or a very common phenomenon which we could call the "smelling salts syndrome" — "I am getting dizzy; I'm going to faint. Get me some smelling salts."

Many famous paintings of aristocratic women show such hands, and one can assume that smelling salts or other medication was an important item in their possession.

3. *Elongated and Excessively Developed Hypothenar Eminence (Mount of Luna)*—As stated previously, the Mount of Luna is an important part of the ulnar (beneath the little finger) zone. It is the reflector of our unconscious energies, our instincts, and our imagination. A large mount is an indication of an accumulation of a large amount of unconscious impulses or energies which are continuously seeking an escape. In other words, the large Mount of Luna is a sign of a piled up unconscious tension. If the zone on the thumb side which represents the conscience or the conscious mind is relatively smaller, the person has trouble handling unconscious tension and will be a potential victim to anxiety neurosis or anxiety attacks.

If the Mount of Luna is encircled by a hypothenar line—so-called line of intuition—the individual's neurotic tendencies are strengthened. To quote Dr. Charlotte Wolff,[3] "The hypothenar

---

[3] *The Human Hand*, p. 140.

Figure 57. *The abundance of crease lines shown on this hand indicates hypersensitivity.*

Figure 58. *There are very few accessory lines on this hand; only the main flexure lines are visible. Such a hand signifies lack of sensitivity.*

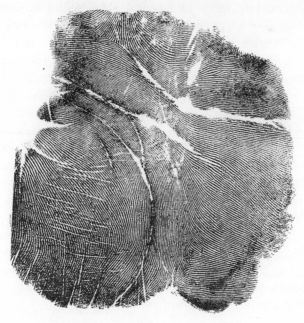

line is the physiological consequence of an over-developed
eminence and this stresses its psychological meaning: over-
developed imagination, the factor which so often causes inadequ-
ate sense of reality and neurotic and hysterical disturbances."

The signs we have just defined indicate *predisposition* to anxiety
neurosis. There are, however, certain hand signs which denote
a state of anxiety—nervous tremor of the fingers, white specks
on the nails, and a cold, clammy hand. During an acute anxiety
state, the individual displays his feelings by restless, neurotic
picking, scratching, stroking, and probing gestures to the face,
hair, and clothing. His hands are constantly in motion and contrast sharply with the hands of a calm, unemotional person.

Coronary Heart Disease

Your body type plays an important part in your predisposition
to coronary heart disease. Young men who have heart attacks
at an early age are generally mesomorphs (overdeveloped muscular system); but the thin, poorly muscled ectomorph rarely has
coronary heart disease before age 40. The mesomorph will gain
more weight between age 25 and 50 than will the ectomorph, and
he will accumulate more cholesterol than will the ectomorph,
which is an important criterion in producing coronary heart
disease. The tendency to gain weight is due not only to the caloric
requirement for energy expenditure but also to the caloric requirement needed in maintaining a large muscle "mass." A classic
patient or victim who may have coronary heart disease at an early
age is the hard-driving, competitive mesomorph between 30 and
50 years old who finds himself so involved in his business activities
that he no longer has any time for exercise or relaxation, except on
occasions that call for eating and drinking. Maintaining or ex-
ceeding his previous caloric intake, but neglecting beneficial exercise, is the fastest way for him to build up cholesterol and fatty
deposits in his blood, tissue, or liver. Healthy outdoor exercise
(such as golfing, biking, tennis) is excellent for prevention of
excessive weight gain for many people; however, for the mesomorph, it can be life-saving for he not only needs this outlet
from a health standpoint but also his particular body type re-
solves tension better through physical activity.

If you are in doubt as to whether you are in this category of "mesomorph," look at your hand. If your hand is round and the palm is firm and muscular, then you have mesomorphic characteristics, even if your body type is a mixture of types. If your heart line is broken or ill-formed beneath the ring finger, I suggest you think about organizing a CPC (coronary prevention club). Abundant accessory lines, which indicate a nervous disposition, and a weak head line, which indicates a poor ability to cope with anxiety or an inability to sublimate frustration, are also key factors to observe in the hand of a mesomorph who wishes to avoid coronary heart disease.

Anxiety is ultimately the most important factor in coronary heart disease both for the mesomorph under 40 and for all body types after 40. A study conducted on a group of coronary patients under the age of 40 reveals that prolonged emotional strain precluded a coronary occlusion in 91 per cent of cases. If extreme anxiety can so severely damage the health of younger men then we can assume that it is doubly damaging for older men.

You can force yourself to diet, to exercise, or to stop smoking, but what about anxiety? Anxiety can be caused by both conscious and unconscious tension. Those things that irritate and frustrate us consciously can be treated because they are obvious. But, unconscious needs and frustrations, which may be even more damaging to our health, are hidden from our conscious minds and therefore go untreated. The key to finding the causes of both conscious and unconscious tension is in the hand.

Palmistry will reveal your predisposition to heart disease, your capacity to cope with tension, and how much tension you suffer and why! You will find out whether you are living in an atmosphere that is compatible with your body type.

Mesomorphic men under the age of 40 are most susceptible to coronary heart disease because of lack of exercise. Ectomorphic and endomorphic men over 40 also are susceptible to heart disease but because of anxiety.

A careful examination of your palm will tell you whether you are mesomorphic and need action when you are disturbed, whether you are endomorphic and need people when you are upset, or if you are ectomorphic and need to be left alone when things are going badly. This body typing tells you how to best handle your emotional problems. If you have not recognized the need to handle them in the proper way for your body type, it is probable that you have added stress instead of decreasing it.

What Your Fingers Can Tell You

In addition, you can tell from the shape of your fingers and fingertips whether you are satisfying your unconscious needs. While there are many desires and goals we strive to fulfill, intangible factors like the need for excitement or routine may be ignored. If your fingers and fingertips show that you are the "square" type, then you must have routine in your life, but if your fingers are spatulate, then you cannot stand routine and must have excitement. Not recognizing and satisfying these needs can result in severe stress, even in individuals who are well adjusted otherwise.

The Case of Executive Stress

This can best be illustrated by stories from my files of men who had the good fortune to find out their needs, adjusted their environments, and achieved better health.

Mr. M was 42 years old and a top executive in a large advertising agency. He consulted me because he had just recently lost his job through a company shakeup and had subsequently developed chest pains which he thought might be evidence of heart disease. The electrocardiogram revealed that he did have some circulatory disturbance in the arteries (coronary insufficiency). I also found that he had high blood pressure and high cholesterol. He was about 20 pounds overweight and he explained this by saying, "You know how it is doctor, I work ten hours a day and at night I'm just too beat to do anything except eat and go to sleep." He was drinking pretty heavily, in addition, and had not played golf or tennis—formerly his favorite sports—for more than five years. His palm revealed that he was a mesomorph with square fingers and nails.

From these facts, I advised him to find another job in a less anxiety-ridden field and to introduce a regimen or routine into his life along with proper diet and exercise or face the possibility of a heart attack. He realized that he was the classic heart-disease-prone patient and wished to save himself, but at first he could not accept the idea of changing his vocation. Instead, he decided to buy a motel in partnership with his father-in-law in Florida with the idea of using this investment as security to give him greater latitude when he chose another job in his profession. He decided to give himself a six-month vacation from the "rat race" and moved to Florida to take over the management of this motel.

I did not see him again for two and a half years, but he told me then that he had never gone back to his former life because of the wonderful adjustment he had found in the new one. He had experienced no more chest pains, had lost weight, was tanned, and looked healthy. He had cut down considerably on his drinking and had greatly reduced his smoking. I was curious to find out just what he had done to effect this marvelous "cure" and he told me the story.

He admitted, "I swim about five times a week in the motel pool; I go to the driving range for an hour on Mondays and Thursdays; on Wednesday I play golf with friends; and on Fridays my wife and I go out to the movies or visiting. The motel keeps me busy most of the week, but I enjoy coping with the problems of running a first-rate place and get considerable satisfaction out of the fact that we have a reputation for excellent accommodations and food. I have a few headaches now and then but nothing I can't handle, and after all, I am the boss."

It's too bad that all of us cannot be as perceptive and wise as this man was. After he realized his needs and the danger he was in, he very intelligently organized his new life so he enjoyed the physical activity he needed and conditioned himself to enjoy this activity in a routine pattern, which he also needed. He followed my advice and now he enjoys not only wonderful good health but also peace of mind. The answer to his problems and yours lies in the hand, but one has to act on the knowledge found there.

A Hotel Owner's Case

Mr. J. owned a hotel for truck drivers. He is a mesomorph with spatulate fingers and found his work extremely limiting. On learning of his needs, he changed jobs and became—of all things—a truck driver. He found that truck driving satisfied him in two ways. The physical activity of driving and unloading a truck gave him the important opportunity to use his body and the excitement of new places and people was satisfying to him emotionally. He too is now a happy man because he heeded the message in his palm.

No discussion of anxiety would be complete without mentioning "love anxiety." Love anxiety can happen at any time but it usually starts in that period during the middle years between 45 and 65. At this time, both men and women begin to have serious doubts about their sexual attractiveness or their ability to perform sexually. Women during menopause may become severely depressed and suffer physical trauma; but, more seriously, the "coronary attack age" for men (between the ages of 40 and 60) exactly coincides with the masculinity crisis or the decline in his sexual powers.

An interesting study showing the importance of virility to good health was conducted by Prof. Jacob Hurwitz of Tel Aviv University and Dr. Elimelech Shamir of Jerusalem Medical School. They studied over 1,200 volunteers representing Jews from many different racial, cultural, and ethnic backgrounds. They found that the Yemeni, or Oriental Jews, enjoyed longevity, virility, and stamina that were the envy of European Jews. Three important factors emerged: better diet, healthier mental attitude, and the fact that before migrating to Israel Yemenite men married teenage girls at intervals of ten years and thereby reinvigorated themselves both sexually and emotionally.

If the modern American male could be relieved of his "love anxiety," perhaps the high mortality rate of 40-to-60-year-old men could be substantially reduced.

With reference to the longevity of Yemenite Jews, we may paraphrase Freud's famous dictum, "in normal sex there is no neurosis" by saying that "with normal sex and love there is no heart attack."

15

The Depth of Love, Libido, and the Line of Heart in the Palm

Modern man can master space and harness atomic energy, but very often he cannot control his psychic energy, that mysterious force known variously as passion, love, or libido.

Despite the large number of articles and books about love and sex, these entities remain mysterious. They will be so, as long as investigators disassociate sexuality from the totality of an individual's behavior.

To understand the total behavior of an imperfect and unpredictable human being, we must know more about his libido, learn more about his constitution and endocrinological (gland) makeup, and, above all, learn about his personality. For, as Dr. Masters and Mrs. Johnson point out in their book, *Human Sexual Response* (p. 301), "Sexuality is a dimension and an expression of personality."

Personality is not a rational or scientific entity in its makeup. Therefore, in addition to rational methods, we sometimes have to use opposite or irrational—or pseudoscientific—means to understand it.

No one knew this better than Freud. He used hypnosis and dream interpretation to understand libido. Not only Freud but

151

his disciple Jung and other students of human behavior used pseudoscience to understand human nature. In ancient times many investigators used palmistry and astrology to understand libido, as do many investigators today. These investigators have an advantage over the empirical scientists in that the "free-wheeling" scientific method in no way limits their thinking, imagination, and intuition, as the conventional scientific approach does.

Another great advantage of palmistry and astrology is that they can be instrumental in obtaining a complete and truthful history from an individual. How many people who would hesitate to tell their doctor their problems with complete candor would withhold information from an astrologer or palmist who could predict their future? Not many. The famed astrologer, Evangeline Adams, who was consulted by world rulers and famous intellectuals, admitted that she learned more from her clients' talk than she did from their horoscopes. This is extremely important in the study of the sexual response, when one must learn the likes and dislikes, the fetishes, the compulsions, and other aspects of an individual.

The handwriting expert experiences this also.

The greatest advantage of the investigation of the hand and handwriting is that one cannot generalize or project his own feelings upon the subject, as many marriage counselors and psychologists do. The approach must be individualistic and objective because no palm print or handwriting is like any other.

To keep the approach to the totality of the individual personalized, many laymen and scientists in the past and present have turned to the hand to gain insight into man's eternal, personal enigma—love and sex.

The young maiden with love anxiety will depend on the petals of the daisy to find the answer to—does he love me or does he love me not? A sophisticated and intelligent female when frustrated will consult a palmist to find the answer to the uppermost questions in her mind—Does he love me? Is he faithful? Will I get married? Will I get a divorce?

To find an answer to these and other related questions, the palmist carefully examines the most important symbol of love—the heart line of the palm. In conjunction with the heart line, the palmist studies the Mount of Venus (barometer of sexuality) and the shape of the little finger or so-called Finger of Mercury.

Heart Line

Krafft-Ebing,[1] famed sexologist, once said that ". . . to woman love is life, to man it is the joy of life. Misfortune in love bruises the heart of the man; but it ruins the life of a woman and wrecks her happiness."

This is why the palmists of India call the line of the heart the life line. V. Ayer[2] feels that the heart line has influence over a person's longevity.

The palmists of India consider the heart line to be paramount, and, unless this line is satisfactory, there is no need to study the palm further. One can understand, then, why, to the Oriental, especially the Hindus, love and sex is the most important factor in life, as is shown by the erotic nature of their temple decorations and by their literature. The Orientals not only believe that sex creates life but also that sex prolongs it.

Based on my lifelong experience with sick and frustrated people, I, too, believe the heart line could be called the line of life. For I am convinced, as are many other physicians, that normal love and sex increase longevity by eliminating many of the stresses and anxieties that shorten life. Little wonder that this most important line derives from the most vital and powerful organ man possesses—the heart.

The heart line, or the upper transverse line, begins at the edge of the palm beneath the little finger, and goes straight across the palm or curves upward, and ends at the base of the middle or index finger.

The short, straight heart line—not running beyond the center of the middle finger—signifies that the individual lacks the capacity to give or receive love and has no strong feelings about his fellowman. If the heart line is long and straight, almost reaching

---

[1] Krafft-Ebing, R., *Psychopathia Sexualist*, Pioneer Pub. N.Y., 1950, p. 15.
[2] Ayer, V. A. K., *Palmistry for Pleasure and Profit*, D. B. Taraporevala Sons & Co., Bombay, 1962.

the other side of the palm, it indicates a tendency toward jealousy and total possession of the object of affection.

When the line terminates upward to the base of the index fingers (Figure 59), it indicates higher types of love. People having this characteristic tend to idolize the love object. And, if the index finger is long also, the person is not only capable of loving strongly but also demands love in return. Franklin D. Roosevelt's hand had such a heart line and long index finger (Figure 60). But if the index finger is short, the person tends toward sentimentality, and idealism and adoration will be an important part of his love, even if the love is not returned.

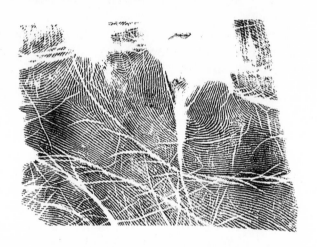

Figure 59. *The heart line terminates at the base of the index finger.*

Heart lines ending at the base of the index finger show love of a more platonic nature, while those terminating at the base of the middle finger (Figure 61, page 156), show more sensual love. If the heart line ends between the base of the middle and the index fingers (Figure 62), it indicates a healthy compromise—a combining of the sensual with the idealistic.

A chained and fretted heart line indicates fickleness and flirtatiousness. If the heart line is bright red, and deep, it shows great passion. A pale and broken heart line indicates a blasé and indifferent person. If the line is forked at the base of the index finger, it heightens the emotionality of the individual and his quality, depth, and direction of love and affection.

To best determine the significance of the heart line, the palmist will compare it with the head line (lower transverse line beneath the heart line). When the heart line is more pronounced than the head line, the urge for affection and love will outweigh all other interests. When the head line is stronger and more pronounced, the love nature is controlled by mental desire (mind over matter we might say). People with this characteristic usually prefer to be alone, or, when they marry, they prefer intellectual rather than sexual companionship.

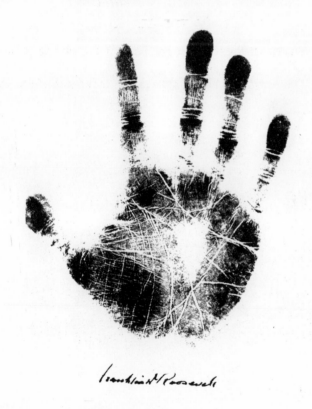

Figure 60. *From the book* Your Hand Tells All *by Alice D. Jennings. Copyright, 1942, by E. P. Dutton & Co., Inc. Reproduced by permission of the publishers.*

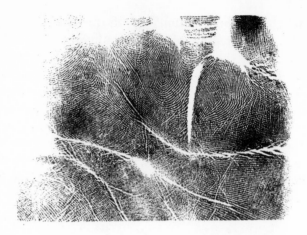

Figure 61. *The heart line ends at the base of the middle finger.*

Figure 62. *The heart line ends between the index and the middle finger.*

The Girdle of Venus

When considering the heart line, one should also evaluate the meaning of the so-called Girdle of Venus—if it is present—because it is sometimes regarded as an adjunct to the heart line. It is a

semicircular crease line running from the base of the index and
the fourth fingers (Figure 63).

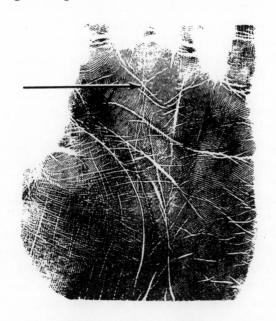

Figure 63. *Types of Venus Girdles.*

As its name implies, the Girdle of Venus is associated with the erotic makeup of the individual. Dr. Wolff points out that palmists are probably right in associating sexual refinement and autoerotic tendencies with the Girdle of Venus. I agree with the opinion of the noted London palmist F. Gettings that this girdle indicates an individual with greater sensitivity. Gettings frequently found this line among drug addicts and other people who need continual and artificial emotional stimulation.

Gettings believes that a short Venus Girdle is a good sign of emotional alertness; it is usually found in show people and other artists known to be easily moved emotionally. On the contrary, the long and broken girdle is a bad sign, indicating a person who cannot find fulfillment for his emotional needs and release from his tensions. Tradition links the Girdle of Venus, whether good or bad in its formation, with strong sexual appetites.

In addition, I associate it with an individual who is extremely sensitive and given to temper tantrums because of his difficulties in finding release for his pent-up nervous energies.

During the last century, when hysteria was very prevalent, the Girdle of Venus was called by many palmists "the line of hysteria." Today we may consider it as the symbol of the frustrated swinger who is unsuccessfully searching for release from his energies in sexual activities. Because this sexual energy is present in both those with hysteria and the modern swinger, I call the Girdle of Venus the line of the libido. Gettings considers it a connection between the external conscious and the internal unconscious qualities of a personality. I consider this sign a bridge between the id (animal) and the ego (human), since I believe as do most palmists, that the ulnar side of the palm represents the unconscious or id, and the radial side the conscious or ego structure.

If the Girdle of Venus is unbroken, it could show a compromise between the id and the ego. If it is broken, libidinal disturbances in the love life might be in evidence; in other words, it may be a symbol of unsatisfied libido.

As we emphasized before, to understand love or libido, we must correlate the heart line and the line of libido with the Mount of Venus and the little finger.

Mount of Venus

Dr. Arnold Kegel, noted gynecologist, has found a positive cor-relation between woman's pelvic musculature and her sexual re-sponsiveness. Women with well-developed and strong pelvic muscles enjoy sex and seldom fail to reach climax. Women with weak pelvic muscles seldom experience orgasm.

Dr. Kegel went so far as to invent a device called the Perino-meter for measuring the muscle tone of the vagina. The woman who is being examined squeezes on a rubber tube inserted in the vagina, and the tube measures the strength of the muscular contraction.

But I don't have to put a woman on an examining table or use the Perinometer to determine whether or not she enjoys sex. All I have to do is examine her handwriting and the musculature of her hand. When a woman applies heavy pressure to her hand-writing and has a well-developed Mount of Venus on her palm, I am quite sure she not only has strong pelvic muscles but also a powerful sexual response. As previously stated, the thumb is the most important part of the human hand; therefore, the mus-cular structure at its base reliably indicates the person's muscular system. It is called the thenar eminence but is more commonly known as the Mount of Venus because it is truly the measure of one's sexuality.

The Mount of Venus is considered to belong to the third part of the thumb. The first phalange of the thumb represents will, the second represents reason, and the third represents the basic energies of the person.

According to Dr. Charlotte Wolff,[3] the Mount of Venus rep-resents the natural driving forces and the instinctive potential of an individual. In the competitions and struggles of daily living, this force constantly seeks escape into action and self-assertion. It can be controlled, however, by the other two phalanges of the thumb, which represents will and reason.

---

[3] *The Human Hand.*

Therefore, the shape of the thumb indicates how an individual can control the most powerful instinct of mankind, sex. The significance of the Mount of Venus is well described by Paul Tabori [4] in his *The Book of the Hand,* "The Mount of Venus represents love, procreation, fecundity. It is enclosed by a long line —like a stream flowing at the base of a hill. This is the life line, for it is Venus and love that begets life: Venus, the goddess of beauty and the mother of love."

If the Mount of Venus is of average elevation and does not have deep lines, an inclination for artistic things, the love of beauty, is signified. If the elevation is very prominent, firm, and red, it denotes that the person has a great love of sex and pleasure. Such a person is vital and warm, and has a zest for all the good things of life—sex, food, art, entertainment, and other diverse interests. According to Benham, these people always marry and rarely commit suicide because life holds too much for them; they count their blessings and dismiss their disappointments without giving in to discouragement.

But, if the mount is small, colorless, and flabby, the person has little energy or interest in sex.

I have observed that an individual with a well-developed Mount of Venus and a strong heart line is not only capable of enjoying life but also makes the effort to learn the art of doing so. He not only has the ability to love but also the capacity to learn how.

The Little Finger

But, an ideal sex partner must know how to do more than make love artfully—he must know how to communicate.

Therefore, to the palmist, the little finger or so-called Finger of Mercury is vital in this connection.

We could call it truly the "messenger of love" since it represents the individual's ability to communicate, especially with the opposite sex. Students of the human hand associate it with the sexual glands and the speech center.

Dr. Charlotte Wolff found short little fingers in a number

---

[4] Chilton Co., Phila. and N. Y., 1962, p. 162.

of paranoid schizophrenics, who are usually underdeveloped emotionally and sexually. She observed that among mongoloids and others with endocrine disturbances the little finger is short and also pointed. These observations led her to conclude that the sex life of an individual is closely associated with the length and shape of the little finger.

My observation was that a woman who has a short pointed little finger (Figure 64, page 162) has an underdeveloped uterus, is very often frigid, and has a low sex drive. In contrast, a long little finger indicates that the sexual apparatus is well developed and the sex drive is strong (Figure 65).

Perhaps the greatest advantage of those having a long little finger is their ability to verbalize their love, to communicate. They can persuade the opposite sex that they are desirable as competent sex and marital partners. Usually they have the gift of acting and diplomacy and encounter few problems in winning their fair ladies. We may assume that Cyrano de Bergerac not only had a long nose but also a long little finger, and that his friend, Christian, who had to get Cyrano to tell the lady of his heart about his great love for her, had a short little finger.

Accordingly, if I were a matchmaker, like those so prevalent in Europe, and someone came searching for a suitable mate, I would look for one with a well-developed little finger, a strong Mount of Venus, and a long and clearly defined heart line.

A question naturally arises—Can a man and woman find marital happiness if they lack one, two, or all three of the qualities just mentioned?

The answer is emphatically yes. But, to bring this about, the pair should be compatible in aspects of life which are basically more important, and certainly more practical, than sexual gratification. The hand can tell us much about this kind of compensatory compatibility and can help us determine whether the husband and wife have compatible temperaments and needs.

The Hand as a Reliable Computer for Compatibility

I am convinced that, if American scientists would realize the value of the hand and handwriting in the study of compatibility between two persons, they would learn that the most reliable

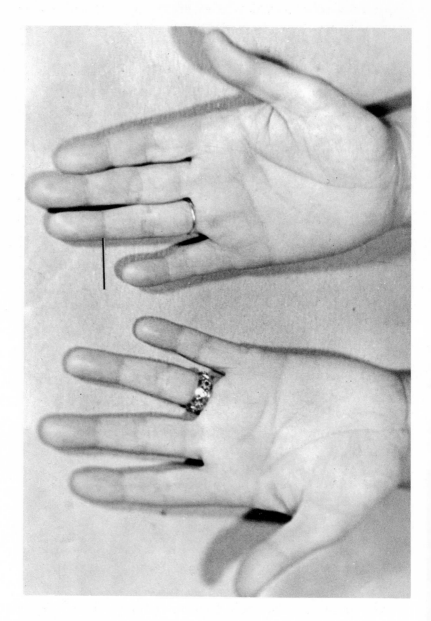

Figure 64. *Short and pointed little fingers. A normally long little finger reaches the joint of the first phalange of the ring finger.*

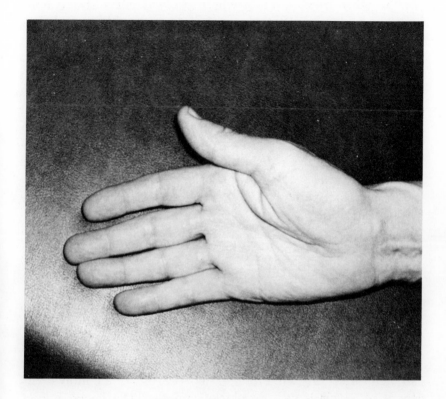

Figure 65. *Long little finger.*

computer is the human hand. For the mechanical computer can select couples based on their known rational likes and dislikes, but it cannot make a computation based on nonrational or subconscious factors — personality makeup, temperament, and certain basic needs such as sexual drive or the urge to power — all of which are of vital importance in the relations between a man and a woman.

From the comparison of the palm print and handwriting of an engaged couple, I have been able to predict, in some cases, that the marriage would end in failure, despite the fact that they were in love and apparently found sexual enjoyment with each other.

On the other hand, in cases where sex was not a strong bond before marriage, I knew that certain couples would have a happy marriage anyway because they were compatible.

For those who are well matched, deep love blossoms easily in the ground of marriage. In my study of adultery, I observed that the more compatible or well-matched the couple is, the less the chances of adultery. This is because sex is not the sole bond; at many times in the course of some marriages it is secondary. However, as compatibility decreases, the importance of sexual satisfaction increases. If a couple can compensate for their inevitable personal differences and emotional makeup and, most important, if they can satisfy each other's basic needs, the chance of adultery and divorce diminishes.

In reference to the most important basic needs, palmistry could find an answer to two vitally important questions: Is the couple undersexed or oversexed? Are they dominating or the dependent type?

Marks of Sensuality

From the Mount of Venus and the shape of the little finger we can determine the sensuality of individuals. If an individual's Mount of Venus is well developed and the little finger is long, he probably is a sensual person. His handwriting usually reveals heavy pressure of downstrokes and cross strokes, fullness of letters, and a long lower loop in such letters as "g" and "y". If the Mount of Venus is flat, the little finger short, and the writing reveals light pressure, light cross strokes, and small lower loops, a lack of sensuality is indicated.

Marks of Domination

A well-developed, long index finger with an enlarged muscular pattern at the base signifies a dominating nature. The handwriting of such a person is characterized by large, elaborate capital letters, especially capital "I". A short index finger, flat Mount of Venus, and small capital letters are signs of a dependent person.

If both husband and wife are undersexed or if both are over-sexed, no problem is likely to arise. A man with a low sex drive will not leave a wife who is not sexually demanding; nor will a highly sexed man leave a wife who is ready for lovemaking at any time.

However important sex may be, often it becomes secondary in a compatible marriage where one partner is dominant and the other submissive or dependent by nature. Couples seldom engage in adultery or get divorced when one who has to dominate to be happy chooses a partner who likes to be dominated. The best results are obtained when one partner is as dominant as the other is submissive.

One does not need to be told what happens when both marriage partners are dominant types. The clash of personalities may be modified by sexual enjoyment of each other, however. As the dominating woman is usually quite vain, she succumbs to a man who lavishes praise and affection on her. When she receives enough attention, she makes an effort to sublimate her dominating nature and quite often succeeds.

But the dominating woman who feels she is neglected is another story. She has frequent explosions of temper. She flirts and may even commit adultery, for she desperately needs to assure herself of her attractiveness. One woman told me that she got much more satisfaction from her lover than she ever did from her husband, "He makes me feel wonderful. He is always there when I want him, and he never ignores a word I say. For him I'm the center of attention, and he never lets me forget it."

The dependent woman could easily be described by associating her with the old-fashioned wife who loves, honors, and obeys. This type is becoming more rare today because we live in a distorted form of matriarchal society where the wife is master and the demoralized and emasculated husband, a slave.

As the wives in our society have become more dominating and aggressive in every aspect of familial living, but especially in sexual aggressiveness, the husbands seem to have retired more and more into the shell of timidity, submissiveness, and dependency. A corollary is that the man becomes sexually disinterested, not only with his wife but with women in general. He comes to feel discomfort and agitation in the company of women, preferring that of men; he likes to be with "the boys" at poker sessions, company or lodge bowling matches, and other exclusively male gatherings. But, the majority of husbands who still like the company of women, will prefer "other" women. They come to regard their wives as nonsexual objects, mothers.

In a society where woman has become the stronger sex and man has become increasingly apathetic, sexually disinterested, and weak, the basic need for dependency or domination in both marital partners becomes irrelevant. The same applies to the sex drive. When a husband is indifferent to sex, it does not matter whether the wife is sex-minded or not.

Therefore, we must seek factors, other than sex or the drive for power, which can make a man and a woman reasonably compatible in marriage. We must also consider that the great majority of marriage partners are a combination of characteristics that tend to make them somewhat average, that is, neither oversexed, undersexed, dominant, nor dependent.

Factors Associated with Love, Sex, and Marriage

Three features closely associated with love, sex, and marriage are: (1) the shape of the hand, (2) the shape of the fingertips, and (3) the starting point of the line of fate. The first two points are more important when studying a man's hand than a woman's, and the third point is more important when studying a woman's hand.

The Square Hand

In the square hand, the palm, the fingernails, and the fingertips are square. The owner of such a hand is "square" indeed. He is conventional and a strict observer of social customs. His life is a matter of routine, order, and system. The same is true of his sex life. It is the same day after day, for this is the way he prefers it — the same time, the same place, the same person, and the same way. The "square" is loyal and seldom commits adultery. If your husband has such a hand, start your marriage with routine, have meals on time, be neat and orderly and don't make him wait.

The Conic Hand

Then there is the conic hand, which is characterized by a triangular shape with tapering fingernails. People with conic hands tend to be impulsive, impatient, sensitive, and easily bored by routine. They respond to harmony, beauty, and artistic surroundings. Their sex lives have sentimental and romantic overtones and they will enjoy sex to the fullest only if the act is surrounded with mood-producing stimuli.

If your husband has this type of hand, you must make it your business to create the mood that inspires love and excitement. Make everything you do seem romantic and appetizing. My strongest advice to you is not to develop a "beauty shop phobia"; remember that you're making yourself beautiful for him, so let him enjoy it.

The Spatulate Hand

The spatulate hand is the easiest type to recognize. The broad fingertips resemble the spatula used by the old-time apothecary in a mortar. The owner of this type of hand is energetic and restless. He loves action, excitement, and adventure and cannot tolerate monotony and restrictions. All this applies equally to his sexuality. If you are old-fashioned and your husband has this type of hand, you are in trouble. He will commit adultery but remember that his infidelities have nothing to do with you or any inadequacy on your part. It is in his nature to seek new experiences and you must tolerate and understand his needs. Keep yourself alive and attractive and learn new tricks as the years go by. He'll keep coming back to you no matter how far he strays.

The Philosophic Hand

The philosophic hand is also easily recognized because of its long palm and long, bony fingers with large joints and long nails. The owner of this hand has an analytical and inquiring mind. He will examine everything, try everything, and then form opinions for himself. Convictions are acquired by this type of person through meditation and analysis. These people are independent and do not depend on hearsay or nonauthoritative statements. Whenever possible they get their information firsthand.

Communication is the key to happiness with a husband who possesses this type of hand. Learn to talk with him about your problems and your feelings, but remember to discuss and not complain.

The Fate Line

The shape of fingers and hands is not as important in women as in men, as women are more adaptable than men. The degree of adaptation is determined by the position of the start of the fate line (vertical line in the center of the palm). If the fate line begins inside the life line or is closely attached to the life line (Figure 66), the woman was greatly influenced by her father and she will transfer these needs, good or bad, to her husband. He should treat her just as a kindly, affectionate father might treat a favored and much-loved daughter.

Figure 66. *The fate line starts inside of the life line.*

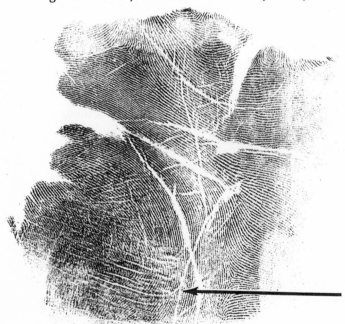

If the fate line starts in the center of the palm, independent of the life line, she will be independent of her husband and he must respect her likes and dislikes. She will be an equal partner, never your slave.

When the fate line rises from the Mount of Luna (Figure 67), she will be greatly influenced by her husband. She is the type who will always love, honor, and obey, but her husband must deserve her devotion and respect her submissive nature.

Figure 67. *The fate line in this print rises from the Mount of Luna.*

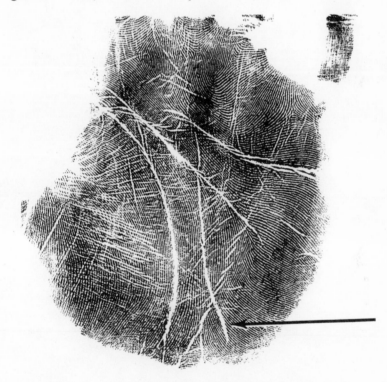

If the fate line stops short of the head line after rising from the Mount of Luna, she is completely submissive and will worship her husband and be his slave no matter how worthless he is. A woman with no fate line is unpredictable. Her husband must have a strong fate line and a strong ego to know how to control her impulsive nature.

Trouble awaits a husband and a wife who both have faulty fate lines or no fate lines at all. If both have strong fate lines, both have the willpower to bring harmony to the relationship.

16

The Fat Girl – What Her Hand Tells

Obesity in the American girl is a serious and sometimes tragic problem. Our national attitude toward fat people in general is that they are unhealthy and ugly, but this attitude is particularly so toward a woman. There are more than subtle pressures brought to bear on her. Not only is it expected that she will not get a husband, but she may not be able to get into the college of her choice or get the job she wants.

This is not because of her lack of qualifications but because of her weight. For instance, I understand that a fat girl will not be hired by the City of New York for the job of "meter maid" in the Traffic Department. Successful applicants for this job need not be "pretty" but they must be trim. Companies which require physical examinations for group insurance consider fat girls generally a risk and hesitate to hire them. Airlines require that hostesses be a certain height and weight and 5 pounds over the limit is usually considered sufficient overweight to cause dismissal from their training program.

These attitudes are somewhat understandable, but not so the

171

fact that the obese girl stands a good chance of being rejected by the college of her choice.

Helen Canning, senior research assistant in nutrition, and Professor Jean Mayer,[1] both of the Harvard School of Public Health, in a study made of two high-ranking colleges, observed that the obese apply to college in about the same proportion as those who are not obese, but they are accepted less frequently. This rejection applies much more frequently to females than to males.

These unjustified hostilities toward the fat girl are especially tragic because, diet regimens notwithstanding, our doctors and our society cannot help these girls. The cures offered by doctors and women's magazines may be effective, but only temporarily. They are good as long as the obese female starves herself. When she resumes normal eating, back comes the excess poundage. An effective part of therapy for obesity must be sympathy. Unfortunately, too many physicians adopt a stern lecture method instead.

This apparently hopeless approach to the problem of the fat girl could be changed if we would study the human hand. It would enlighten us in understanding such contributory factors as the constitutional, endocrinological, and psychological influences of obesity. And it would help us understand the fat girl as a whole person.

Pituitary obesity represents only a small percentage of obesity, so we will not dwell on this aspect at any length. In passing, I would like to point out that one can recognize pituitary obesity from the hand and tell whether the pituitary obesity began when the subject was a child or an adult. In juvenile pituitary obesity there are fat pads on the back of the hands and the back of the second and third phalanges of the fingers. The first phalange, however, is slender and tapering. In adult pituitary obesity we find an elongation of the hand, the fat pads are not present, and the fingers do not taper.

In an article in the *Journal of the American Medical Association*,[2] Carl Seltzer and Jean Mayer stress the importance of the

---

[1] Canning, H. and Mayer, J.: "Obesity — Its Possible Effect on College Acceptance." *New England Journal of Medicine*, Nov. 24, 1966.

[2] "Body Build and Obesity — Who Are the Obese?", *JAMA*, Aug. 31, 1964, pp. 677-684.

role of constitutional factors in obesity, "Obesity occurs in greater frequency in some physical types than others." Seltzer and Mayer stated, "It was found that in every single instance, the bony dimensions of obese girls were significantly greater than those of nonobese girls and in relation to stature..." They reached this significant conclusion, "The data also showed quite dramatically that the hands of obese girls [are] broader than those of the nonobese in absolute dimensions and considerably shorter and broader in relative proportions." [3]

The human hand will help us clarify the three basic components in the relationship between body build and obesity. The first component is characterized by softness and roundness; the second is characterized by a combination of bone and muscle development; and the third component is characterized by linearity and fragility.

The mesomorphic hand has well-developed, firm, muscular patterns and it is pink. These people love eating; but, in contrast to the endomorph, they love action, adventure, sports, and outdoor life. Therefore, they have a perfect balance of caloric intake and expenditure. However, when they get older, or when they cannot be as active, they may continue to eat their usual diet and get fat.

The fat girl usually has an endomorphic hand. The endomorphic hand is short, broad, flat, flabby, and wide with sausagelike fingers. This hand shows that the subject loves to eat and is lazy. She craves affection and company, and, if she is left alone, will seek escape in food.

Those Who Will Never Be Thin

The first step in helping an endomorph realize good emotional health is for her to recognize that she will *never be thin*! From her hand she will know that she is destined to be round and soft and prone to overweight. By permanently regulating her diet, by cutting down on food intake but *not* cutting food out, and by establishing a regular routine of exercise and activity she will keep her weight within attractive limits. She must accept the fact that

---

[3] *Annals New York Academy of Sciences*, Vol. 134, Art. 2, pp. 497-1066.

fad diets and diet pills are not for her. She might lose weight temporarily but inevitably she will gain back this weight and more. The idea is not to become resigned to being fat but to accept the advantages of being "pleasantly plump."

To accomplish her new outlook and new approach to living, she needs the moral support of her family and friends. She also needs sympathy. A Chicago specialist in obesity, Dr. James Hutton,[4] has proposed a "Be Kind to Fat Folks Week . . . a week that should last throughout the year." In his study of life histories of overweight patients, Dr. Hutton was impressed by the relation of emotional insult to the onset of obesity. He stated that children who move from a neighborhood where they have friends to another where they have none, many times become obese. He mentioned also that children are very unkind to each other, and practically all fat people need moral support of some kind — some need only that.

The Value of Palmistry to the Fat Girl

The greatest value of palmistry is that it can offer positive and effective psychotherapy to the hopeless, unwanted, fat girl. The palmist can offer hope to the fat girl because, unlike most physicians, his reaction to her condition is not controlled by the scales, which can deal with no factor but her weight in pounds. His main interest is to learn whether her life line is good, her head line reveals a good mental attitude, and her heart line reveals a happy sex life.

Dr. Alvin Feinstein of Yale University, a top expert on obesity, is of much the same opinion. In a panel discussion sponsored by the American College of Physicians in New York he said that losing weight is not as important as getting well psychologically and sexually. He feels there is no doubt that weight reduction is directly beneficial to a person with cardiopulmonary disease or diabetes, but there is no unequivocal scientific data that loss of weight will prevent a perfectly healthy fat person from getting sick. If a person is 20 or 30 pounds overweight, and is otherwise

---

[4] Meeting of Illinois State Hygienist Society — 1967.

well and getting along psychologically and sexually, Dr. Feinstein feels there is no proof that it is necessary to impose a diet.

A competent palmist is aware of these facts. From the life line he can reassure the obese girl that she can live as long as the slender girl, and from the heart line he can tell her if she can be as happy in her sex and love life as the glamor girl — who often is *not*.

Palmistry can also answer two pertinent questions asked of Albert J. Stunkard,[5] famous obesity expert:

(1) Is it true that obese people are usually jolly and good-natured?

All the characteristics of an individual, including virtues, are written in the hand. Whether the obese person is really jolly and happy or only covering up her hostility will be revealed. A truly happy, obese woman has come to terms with her destiny and, if she has not, she can be made aware of it and her hostility can be obviated.

(2) Why is obesity in a woman so often associated with mother-liness and sustenance?

From my observation, the handwriting and the hands of obese women show that they are warmhearted, friendly, extroverted, affectionate, tolerant, and loving wives. Maternity agrees with them physically and psychologically and they make understanding mothers.

However, I have observed that many fat girls suffer from a psychoneurosis which causes them to develop a distorted body image and hostility toward themselves and the men who ignore them. This neurotic disturbance is fostered in childhood and carried over into adult life. A distorted body image is the difference between a happy endomorph and an unhappy endomorph. A distorted body image means a neurotic preoccupation with the negative aspects of obesity frequently to the exclusion of other personal characteristics.

A good palmist will show a woman with a distorted body image

---

[5] *The Encyclopedia of Mental Health,* Vol. 4, A Div. of Franklin Watts, Inc., 1962—Albert Deutsch, Editor-in-Chief, Helene Fishman, Executive Editor.

that she can be a good mother, so essential in a world where there are so many disturbed children. She can be shown that she can be a good wife, giving comfort and warmth to a man who may have been emasculated by a glamor girl or his demanding mother. And, the palmist can show her that she can compete successfully with the spoiled, narcissistic glamor girl by learning to "love, honor and obey."

A Happy Ending to One Fat Girl's Romance

This young girl was a happy endomorph, lovely but overweight, and only 22 years old. She came to me about her love life, the only trouble spot in an otherwise happy life. This girl had a lovely apartment, a good job, many friends, and a beautiful roommate whom she liked very much but felt inferior to physically. They both entertained quite a bit and she had fallen in love with one young man, the most frequent visitor to their apartment. She rightly suspected that this attractive young man confided in her and asked her advice so frequently because he was secretly in love with her roommate.

I told her that her hand showed a strong head line, a well-developed Mount of Venus, and a good heart line. Therefore, she had many excellent qualities for attracting and satisfying a mate. She was not interested in marriage since her present status satisfied her needs but she did want the love of this particular young man. I reassured her that if she were patient and continued to be warm and outgoing with this man *she would eventually win his heart.*

She called me tearfully some months later and announced that her roommate and her friend had eloped together. The secrecy was part of their plan not to "hurt her feelings." I sympathized with her on this unhappy turn of events, but I again counseled her to be patient and not to hold a grudge against either of her friends. From periodic conversations over the next two years she kept me informed of her doings and her excellent progress in following my advice. I was not surprised to hear one day that her former love had returned to her after a divorce had ended his marriage to the "glamor" girl. My "fat" friend is now this man's wife! In addition, she has the respect of her former roommate who comes to her frequently to ask her advice about her unhappy love affairs. This "fat" girl is still overweight, but she has the irresistible glow of a fulfilled and happy woman, one who not only receives but also gives love.

The Case of Another Fat Girl

Another girl who responded to a palmist's skill was Annette. Like most fat girls she felt rejected, depressed, and unhappy. Her only solace was food, a well-known substitute for love. I studied her handwriting and palm prints when she visited my office, and I assured her that she had a chance for a happy, healthy, sex-fulfilled future. I predicted that within two years she would get married, but I cautioned her not to jeopardize her chances by overeating.

Eleven months later, Annette called to tell me that she was engaged. I wasn't surprised that my prediction had come true. What amazed me was that she had lost 23 pounds and looked radiant — from 165 down to 142 pounds!

"How did you do it?" I asked, and she answered, "I stopped worrying, stopped overeating, and began living."

"A starvation diet, diet pills?" I asked.

"No, I don't go hungry but I eat a lot less than I used to. I dance more, walk more, work vigorously when cleaning the apartment, and when I cook I'm not concerned whether it's harmful to me or not but whether my fiancé enjoys it. Perhaps the secret of my weight loss is that I wasn't concerned about myself but about making my fiancé happy. I just wanted to look good and please him."

I concluded, "In other words you were more interested in 'seducing' than reducing."

17

Palmistry as a Key to the Problem Drinker

In the United States today 5 million souls are statistically considered alcoholics. Alcoholics are individuals whose addiction to alcohol is considered chronic and has rendered them useless to society and themselves. This astronomical figure represents only 6 per cent of the total drinking population of this country. Of this 6 per cent, only 3 per cent or half the alcoholics, represent the "skid row" bum alcoholic. The other 3 per cent is made up of "nice" people from all walks of life, all ages, and all economic strata. These "nice" people all have one thing in common with the derelict, the "skid row bum." At one point in their lives they were all "social" drinkers. They did not become addicts overnight, unlike narcotics addicts who sometimes become addicted very rapidly and hopelessly. Whether the long haul ended in a gutter, a vacant lot, a state hospital, a private or public psychiatric ward, or an expensive "drying out place" in the country, they came there by pretty much the same route with approximately the same loss of self-respect.

At some point in the life of every alcoholic there was a "crossroads" where the heavy or chronic drinker could have been salvaged. We are interested in the drinkers who are standing at this

179

crossroads now and those who have a friend or a relative who could be helped. This book does not have the scope necessary to cover the "cures" espoused by various doctors and research groups; rather, we will try to show the methods we have learned that are useful in determining the danger and preventing the further addiction of those we call problem drinkers. Problem drinkers are not yet alcoholics. They are aware that they drink too much too often and that their drinking is causing them trouble in their jobs and personal lives. Many times they are aware that they drink compulsively with dire results and that they drink too much after solemn resolutions just to have one. Their drinking problems have become known to other people and usually someone has had the courage to discuss the possibility of "alcoholism" with the individual.

However, the problem drinker does not feel that he is an alcoholic or even a potential alcoholic and alibis with the familiar phrases, "I can take it or leave it," or "I can quit any time I want to," or "A sociable drink never hurt anybody." These empty words cover up the nagging doubts left by one too many hangovers, blackouts, and humiliating performances. But, every heavy drinker who has to resort to these subterfuges knows deep inside that he has a problem and needs help. What he often does not recognize is that his best bet for help is self-help while the problem is in the "heavy" stage and before it has progressed to the last, desperate stage of chronic alcoholism.

Steady day-in and day-out drinking is the most boring and unproductive activity in the world. No one has ever suggested that drunks have an interesting life. The infantile preoccupation with oral satisfaction in the form of anesthetizing liquid is not interesting or fulfilling and has yet to produce anything other than grief for the individual and for society. This being the case, why do so many potentially useful people choose to spend their lives doing it?

The answer is usually they cannot help it. Not that they cannot stop doing it—but because they do not know why they are doing it, they are unable to muster the strength and motivation to allow themselves freedom from a destructive habit.

There are those who say that drinkers are seeking ` God" in a bottle and experts who claim that they suffer from a "disease." Others say alcoholism is a convenient "escape" from a hostile, dog-eat-dog society—in other words, it is society's fault. Whatever their theories though, they all agree that alcoholics have certain negative personality traits in common with other neurotic types who do not become alcoholics.

Hand Signs of the Potential Alcoholic

In our study of the hand, the potential alcoholic is definitely one who could profit most from the revelations found there. He can discover whether or not he has these negative traits:

1. *Inner conflicts or unresolved psychosexual difficulties* — shown by a broken Girdle of Venus;
2. *Feelings of insecurity and inferiority* — characterized by an underdeveloped, short index finger;
3. *Low tolerance to stress and frustration* — extreme rigidity or flexibility of fingers;
4. *Dependency* — shown by lack of fate line or of fate line that starts on or near the life line;
5. *Hostility* — shown by coarse-textured skin, rigid fingers, extreme red color, short thumb, or abnormal dermatoglyphics or atavistic (simian) line;
6. *Lack of self-expression or ability to communicate* — short little finger;
7. *Lack of willpower or self-determination* — characterized by lack of fate line or weak or short thumb.

In my practice as a doctor on Chicago's north side "Bughouse Square" area, I have treated many human derelicts and among the hundreds whose hands I have examined I have yet to see a "strong" hand. However, enough of them have the above qualities to convince me that my observations are correct. While these signs do not necessarily indicate alcoholism in themselves, these negative traits in combination with other factors could tip the balance of an individual toward an addiction to alcohol.

I have known heavy or even chronic drinkers who have some of the adverse signs present in their hands who could control their drinking when necessary, but invariably they had other signs in their hands (such as strong life or head lines or strong fate lines) which served to counterbalance the weak tendencies in their psychological makeup.

Significance of the Fate Line in Alcoholism

The significance of a fate line, and in particular a strong fate line, cannot be emphasized enough. For example, below are the palm prints of two men who have severe drinking problems. As you can see in Figure 68 there is a strong fate line while in Figure 69 there is none.

Their stories are good examples of the significant difference this line makes. Coincidentally, both men are writers and are highly gifted and accomplished in their field. Drinker No. 1, however, is able to curtail his drinking for long periods whenever he starts to worry that he is drinking too much.

Drinker No. 2 has a different story. He tells it this way, "I became an alcoholic when I had my first half ounce of whisky and staggered down the street pretending to be drunk — and hence mature and sophisticated. I wanted to show off, be the center of attention . . . dramatize myself — and I still tend to dramatize myself." While he categorized himself an alcoholic, I believe he would be considered a problem drinker rather than an alcoholic since he does manage to stay sober long enough to support his handicapped wife and himself. Even though he has been drinking to excess for more than 40 years, he is still a periodic drinker who can stop when the necessity to earn money appears imperative. He, himself, recognizes his lack of willpower and determination as shown by his lack of a fate line. This is his own analysis of the situation:

> "All of my adult life I have been objectively aware of an almost total lack of willpower and perseverance, except in the area of educational effort. My effort here endured for years and was extraordinary for the daily hours spent in study — my ego demanded that I attain the status of a classical scholar. I never courted a girl in my life unless she reacted favorably from the start and I never fulfilled an unpleasant obligation that required time and patience until I was in my fifties."

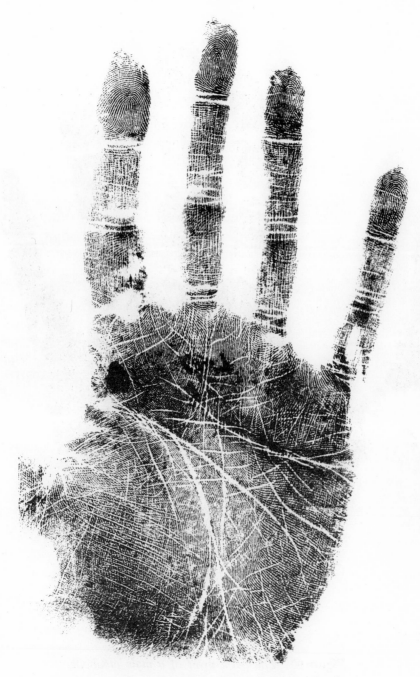

Figure 68. *The palm print of a male heavy drinker.*

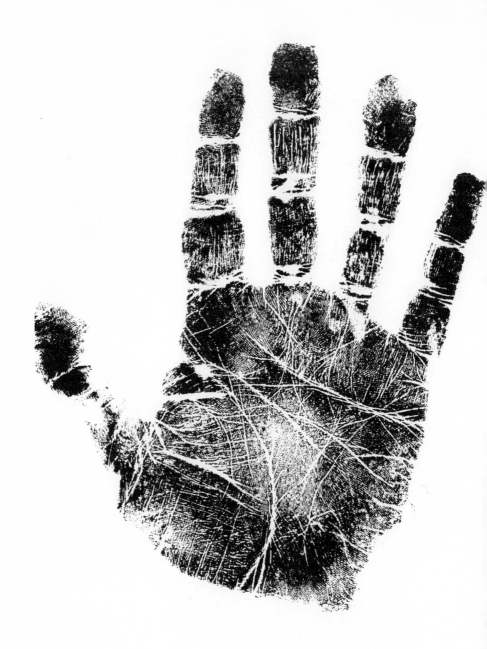

Figure 69. *The palm print of a male alcoholic.*

Here we have a clear picture of an individual with strong qualities for success. He has a strong life line, and an excellent head line, which should have given him an edge to start with, but without a strong determination, (lack of fate line), plus the psychosexual disturbances shown by a broken Girdle of Venus, he has not developed his potential but wasted it.

Drinker No. 1 has had his problems too, as shown by the Girdle of Venus. But since he does have a strong fate line, he has been more successful as a writer and as a functioning human being than Drinker No. 2 because he has the willpower to stop hurting himself. He could, if he chose, stop drinking altogether without too much effort. *Drinker No. 2 will never be cured of his dependency on alcohol but can only hope to arrest it periodically.* Because of their strong constitutions, these men have been able to sustain the consumption of tremendous amounts of alcohol for many years without suffering from physical ailments that usually accompany overindulgence.

Significance of the Life Line in Alcoholism

The constitution line or life line is important in determining how much alcohol a person can take and how he will react physically from too much drinking. The following story illustrates the importance of this line.

At a party, a friend of mine who was concerned about her husband's drinking asked me to read his palm, knowing that he would never consent to be examined by a doctor about his drinking. I looked at his hands and noticed he had clubbed fingers and extremely pale fingernails. In addition, he had a very weak constitution line broken in several places. I asked him if he had had any previous heart or lung disorder, since these signs are symptoms of these ailments. He answered no. I inquired whether he was a heavy drinker and commented that drinking could also be a reason for these physical signs. He replied that he was a "Churchill" type of drinker ... "heavy but controlled." I then explained to him that he was not a strong type physically but, on the contrary, he was a potential alcoholic and his health would surely be affected if he continued to drink heavily. I explained that even heavy drinkers have broken down after many years of controlled drinking to become alcoholics and that the experts do not know why this is, any more than they can pinpoint the elusive factor that makes one person more susceptible to dependence on alcohol than others. He pooh-poohed my warnings and evidently continued to drink in the "Churchill" fashion for another two years. Then, as I predicted, he developed cirrhosis of the liver. By this time, of course, he had harmed himself beyond repair physically. He had harmed himself emotionally too because he now was confronted with a serious disease and the withdrawal of a much needed emotional support — alcohol.

A Case of Fearing Inherited Alcoholism

Another, more encouraging instance was when a very worried young woman consulted me because she was afraid she might become an alcoholic like her father had been. This girl had real cause for concern since, although she had not taken her first drink until she was 26 (she was 30 years old at this time), she had now become a compulsive drinker. At the time she consulted me she was not drinking heavily with any frequency, but she drank to oblivion during periods of anxiety. Recently a very frightening incident happened during one of these drinking sprees, and she had been hospitalized with a concussion. She had regained consciousness in restraints and was told she had been found lying in a pool of blood outside a restaurant. She could not remember having been there or anything that had happened, not even the people she had been with that night.

A hospital psychiatrist examined her and refused permission for her to leave the hospital without a psychiatric examination. She panicked at the thought of being locked up in a psychiatric ward, but kept her surface calm enough to convince the doctor that she should be released. He finally agreed, and this woman, once she was free, decided to get help from me since a good friend of hers was a patient of mine.

I examined her and found both good and bad signs. In the left hand (Figure 70-a) she had many islands in the heart line; this shows a tendency to be emotionally confused and unable to love successfully. In the right hand (Figure 70-b), however, the heart line showed fewer and smaller islands than the left hand, indicating that she could overcome her predisposition to emotional disturbance.

In the left hand, the head line showed a large island, indicating mental disturbance and confusion. The head line in the right hand had a smaller island than the one in the left. Both palm prints showed no abnormal dermatoglyphics; i.e., highly placed axial triradius. There were no whorls or other patterns on the Mount of Venus or the Mount of Luna. Although there was a break in the life line in the left hand, there was none in the right hand, indicating physical strength and endurance. The indications were that she was constitutionally strong and genetically well formed.

The most interesting discovery, however, was the three fate lines in the right hand; there was only one in the left hand. The fate line in the left hand was more deeply marked and stronger than any in the right hand. I interpreted this to mean that, as a child, this woman had had strength and determination but had recently developed a low tolerance to frustration. She confirmed this by telling me that when she was a little girl and had suffered the humiliation of being the daughter of an alcoholic she had developed a terrific drive to get out of her environment. She decided that she must know more than anybody else and educated herself far beyond any of her family. She had spent almost all of her spare time devising plans and schemes to leave her sordid surroundings. She finally made her "escape" and achieved a good life far away from her former home. However, she fell in love with a man who treated her badly and left her abruptly for another woman. She found herself unable to cope with this event and started to drink. She drank moderately at first, "just to dull the pain," but eventually her drinking evolved into the pattern we have described.

In short, this young woman had lost her purpose in life, her direction. The heart line in her right hand showed that she could love more wisely and more satisfactorily in the future. Added indications were that, although the strongest fate line of the three in her right hand joins the life line (showing that she was definitely influenced by her environment — searching for a father

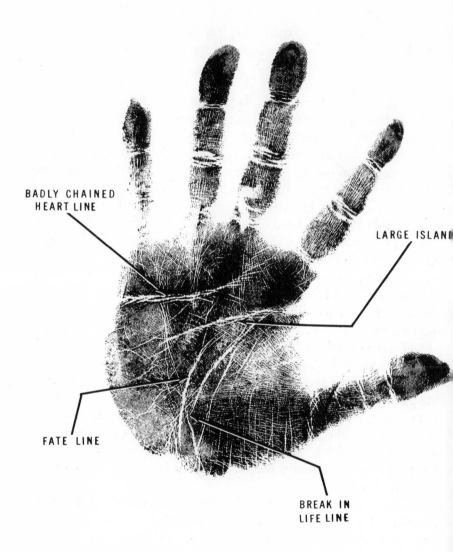

BADLY CHAINED
HEART LINE

LARGE ISLAN

FATE LINE

BREAK IN
LIFE LINE

Figure 70-a. *The left hand of a compulsory, woman drinker.*

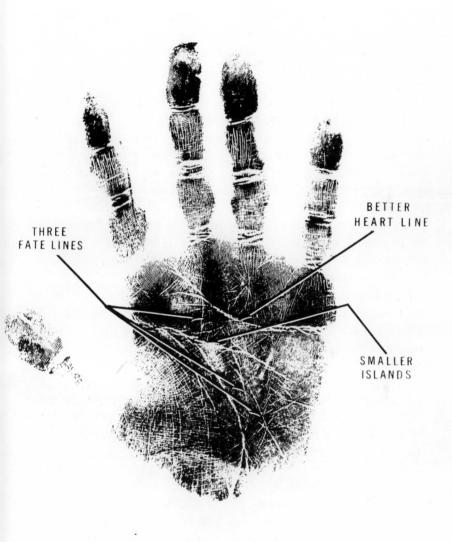

Figure 70-b. *Right hand of the same person in Figure 70-a.*

image), there is another fate line which starts from the Mount of Luna, meaning she will eventually meet a man who will cure her of her need for a substitute for her father.

Furthermore, if she improves her negative traits, which her right hand shows she could, she will not become an alcoholic. For instance, she had a long little finger, which indicates a high ability to communicate with other people. She had no broken Girdle of Venus — and this was what she was particularly interested in hearing — meaning she had no psychosexual difficulties. This, as we have already mentioned, is a strong sign that the individual can withstand an alcoholic predisposition. In addition, although the palm print does not show it, her palm is square with the fingers nearly flat on top. This is a definite indication that her life should involve considerable routine. She had led a very unsettled and insecure existence up to this point and had probably added to her problem of anxiety by not satisfying her need for a settled, secure, and routine home life. Another good sign was a strong index finger. We know this means that she will inevitably master her destiny, good or bad.

I explained all these things to her and made clear that she must regain that early determination and purpose in life. "The trouble," I said, "is that you have achieved some goals and have not replaced them with new ones. From your hands you are obviously a person who must have clear and concise goals to work toward. When you find them you will not need to drink at all."

I also counseled her that she must develop her superego or conscience (weak fate line) in order to combat her negative traits. By this I meant that she must develop a philosophy about life, her work, and her love life which would sustain her in critical times and help her withstand frustration. I concluded that three weak fate lines signified lack of determination, no sense of purpose, and a weak superego. If she could not achieve a purpose in life by her own efforts, perhaps she could find an answer in some religious philosophy, if not in an organized religion.

The last time I heard from her, she was a much happier person, although she still had drinking bouts when extremely depressed mentally. She did drink on occasion, she said, but assured me that they were of one night's duration and never to the point of passing out. Her love life was still turbulent but she had made great strides mentally. She had approached her career with new vigor and, better still, she had a more routine, stable life.

Answers to Alcoholism in the Palm

The heavy drinker who wants to fill his life, who wants to live his life fully will find the answers written in his palm. Every man or woman has individual reasons for drinking and the remedies to their problems must also be individual. Each palm is unique and the mirror of a particular personality; therefore, it is a good map for discovering the "way" for a particular individual. The heavy drinker must carefully examine his hand or be helped to examine it for negative factors to overcome and positive factors that will help him.

The most important indicator is the life line. If this line is weak, faulty, or short, the owner must realize that he has a weak constitution. Since alcohol has a damaging effect on even strong constitutions, it is undeniable that its effects must be disastrous for those with a weak constitution or weak body chemistry. Another important sign is an alteration in the appearance of the skin and nails. This sign indicates that something is wrong with the body chemistry and, here again, alcohol could prove fatal.

If one parent was alcoholic and the other was not, you could compare the palm prints of each with your own and determine which of the parents' your own palm resembles. If you had a disturbed childhood or if your parents were heavy drinkers or alcoholics, these circumstances should be taken as a warning that you could have a congenital predisposition to alcohol intolerance, and promptly curtail any drinking you do. If you have trouble communicating with other people on a meaningful level unless you have had something to drink and/or if you have the other signs in the hand we mentioned, you should give serious thought to your future.

Palmar Clues to Need for Spiritual Help

Perhaps there will be those who feel they are too sophisticated to accept religious or moralistic methods. And, while it is true that penitence, prayer, and charity are religious terms and the basis of most religious and ethical systems, they are practical methods for heavy drinkers. If a rejection of religion or morality has brought you to the point where you have no life that is not seen through an alcoholic haze, then your thinking has been wrong somewhere.

The hand offers some clues as to the need of a religious experience in the life of the individual. If the space between the person's heart line and head line is narrow, he needs a religious experience no matter what his current views are. If his head and heart lines are widely separated, he does not need an actual religious experience as much as he needs to seek and find the faith in himself that he has lost along the way. Chances are he is drinking heavily because he has not developed his potentialities. If there is a mystic cross between his head and heart lines, then mysticism and not alcohol is his "religious" remedy. If he has a well-developed line of Sun and third finger then he should find more relief in artistic endeavors than in alcohol. If he has a square hand and a narrow space between the head and heart lines, then an old-fashioned religion is for him. If he has a philosophic hand with knotty fingers, well-developed joints, and long nails, he should examine all religious philosophies and find a sustaining belief. If he has a spatulate hand with widely separated fingers and a wide space between the head and heart lines there will be no old-fashioned religion for him.

But, whatever the method of salvation may be — whether it is religious or otherwise — any method that brings an individual's life into proper focus and gives meaning to his days should be sought out through penitence, prayer, and charity. If these terms make one nervous, then say ventilation, introspection, and re-education and persuasion. Whatever you call them, they work for everyone with a drinking problem regardless of childhood, parents, current situation, or problems.

New Horizons for the Recovered Alcoholic

One question a heavy drinker might think but never say is, "What am I going to do with all this sober time." The answer to this question lies in the hand. We have already described the various body types and the activities that each enjoys. One could start there by determining what area is the most promising for his particular body type. If he is a mesomorph, he may want to pursue some sport or activity which requires lots of action to burn up excess energy, or he may discover, along with an interest in a sport, a leaning toward art or music. He can pursue them both, substituting them for liquor. In addition, he will even find a place in his life for the consideration of others. It is inevitable that, when he is involved in something which excites him and he experiences a fuller existence he will find people to be more interesting and also interested in him.

The endomorph will probably find his pursuits in less active realms but should make an effort to meet people with similar interests and diversify his activities so that he does not spend too much time alone. He must always be among people.

The ectomorph has great potential for becoming absorbed in solitary activities and, as long as the absorption is sufficient, there is no return to unhealthy drinking problems. Becoming fanatical about music or art is still definitely preferable to excessive drinking.

It is no more improbable to look for answers in the hand than to look for them in a bottle of liquor. If one looks to the hand for answers and to himself for strength to change his life, one will find that it is easier than he ever dreamed possible.

18

The Middle-Age Crisis
as Shown in the Hand

In dealing with anxiety, we have covered problems ranging from obesity to alcoholism and analyzed the importance of the hand in relation to these problems. We will now deal with a problem in anxiety which has a particular application to the American male in general — the anxiety of aging, or the phenomenon of the middle-age crisis.

The middle-age crisis in men has been compared to a woman's change of life, but the comparison is not a realistic one. A woman's change of life is physical and involves the decrease in function of a reproductive organ. After a period of discomfort and proper treatment with hormones, the body adjusts to the changes that are taking place. However, a man is attacked psychologically with dramatic changes in his most vulnerable areas — his self-image and his ego.

Most men work hard to provide for their families, accept responsibilities at a young age, and compete in a dog-eat-dog society to achieve their goals. They are not accustomed to deep feelings of inadequacy or to sharing their worries or problems with their wives or families. American men, especially, are taught to act stoically towards life and to accept rebuffs and disappointments without revealing their mental anguish. It is not considered masculine to complain about hardship. And, most men are not aware that they will go through a middle-age crisis. Therefore, when it does begin, he may feel that he alone has this terrible burden to bear. He is unprepared for the sudden realization that he is considered an old man, a forgotten man, while he is still in his prime. Of course, physically and mentally he is not an old man. It is true that he is aging, but he is not old and in many instances he has just begun to hit his stride. The middle-aged man is important in every culture, but in America it is different. The youth cult, or worship of youth, is a common occurrence in this country; therefore, a man reared in this culture feels, or is made to feel, old before his time.

We have discussed how valuable knowledge gained from the hand can be to individuals suffering from obesity or alcoholism. The hand can be just as valuable, if not more so, in helping individuals who face middle-age crisis.

Five Important Hand Signs in Middle Age

We have shown that the hand of the individual holds the clues to his basic personality, his needs, his potential, and the indications of his destiny. The five important hand signs in discussing the middle-age crisis are: (1) the index finger, (2) the thumb, (3) the Mount of Venus, (4) the life line, and (5) the fate line and the line of Sun. These will be described below.

The *index finger* indicates the development of ego or, that which deals with his outward life, his ambitions, strength of will, and power of dominance. The index finger and *the thumb* are always considered in conjunction with each other since the thumb is the measure of a person's ability to carry out his goals or ambitions.

The *Mount of Venus* is considered in conjunction with the life line because the Mount of Venus indicates the interest and drive of the individual in physical matters, particularly the sex drive.

The *life line* is an indication of the vitality or constitution of the individual, or the amount of energy or physical stamina which is at his disposal to satisfy his drives.

The *fate line* and *line of Sun* are considered together because the fate line is an indication of the adaptability of the individual and of his determination, while the Sun line, if one is present, acts as a sister line and strengthens the fate line.

We have not previously mentioned the line of Sun, or the "line of success," because it has a special significance for the middle-aged person. This line indicates success in life regardless of age; that is, a person can be successful after middle age if he has a line of Sun that ends at the base of the third finger. This portion of the hand represents old age. The palm print shown in Figure 71 is a good example.

Figure 71. *The fate line in this hand ends at the heart line, but the line of Sun ends at the base of the third finger.*

The palm print of this man shows a strong fate line and a strong line of Sun. The fate line ends near the heart line, representing the early fifties—a time when most men lose their drive or ability to succeed. However, the line of Sun ends at the base of the third finger, showing that age cannot stop his drive for success.

Generally, if the majority of these signs are well developed, the individual will grow old gracefully or make a successful adjustment to a downward trend of activity or responsibility. He will have the ability to adapt to changing circumstances. If a majority of these signs are weak or faulty, he may age prematurely or begin to act and look like an old man. He may also begin to suffer psychosomatic illnesses, neurotic reactions, insomnia, alcoholism, or the loss of virility.

Incidental to this discussion, it should be pointed out that women, also affected by the mania for youth and beset with problems of aging, have the advantage of being able to prolong the illusion of youth longer than a man. They may resort to countless artifices such as face lifting, cosmetics, and fashion to preserve their youthful image. In addition, women mature sexually just as a man begins his sharpest decline. Since a man's sexuality is so closely tied to his psychological makeup, he usually faces the loss of his physical attractiveness along with a decline in his sexual vigor. He has the added burden of an ego that is badly shaken by the "emptiness" of middle age.

There can be no discussion of middle age without consideration of the crisis which occurs, or the concern with virility which plays such a prominent part in this phenomenon. Dr. David Swartz[1] professor of urology at the University of Manitoba, in a paper entitled "Sexual Difficulties after 50: The Urologist's View," suggested, "In assessing sexual difficulties one should distinguish between growing old and aging. Growing old is a process of maturing, is progressive, and results in a natural slowdown. To age, however, is pathological and therefore regressive. Given the right heredity, hormonal pattern, and nutrition, sexual power is no more weakened in man by advancing years than are other bodily functions."

---

[1] *Canadian Medical Assn. Journal,* Jan. 29, 1966, Vol. 94.

We will show that the hand mirrors not only heredity, hormonal pattern, and nutrition, but also the totality of the individual, which is after all the true measure of sexuality and its expression. Here, the value of palmistry is unquestionable because it offers an understanding of what the middle-age crisis means to the individual himself and a method of combating the "emptiness" of middle age.

The palm of the hand is a map that helps the individual negotiate the wilderness of middle age. I discovered this myself over 20 years ago when I went through the middle-age crisis. I have spent the past 20 years happy and productive because I discovered palmistry and its importance to middle age, just as medical science is discovering its importance as a diagnostic tool today. But, every middle-aged man does not have to go to a palmist as I did to discover his potential, he can do it himself with a little guidance, a little patience, a lot of understanding, and some study. If he wishes, he can make his middle years not only productive but also rewarding, even exciting! Following are significant guides for your consideration.

Index Finger and Thumb

The length of the index finger can be measured by the third finger. If it is as long as the third finger, you have a long index finger, if it is shorter than the third finger by a noticeable amount, you have a short index finger. If your index finger is considerably longer than the third finger, you have the so-called finger of Napoleon; it was named this because the famous Corsican general was said to have this type of long index finger.

A long index finger is usually accompanied by a thumb of proportionately the same size and strength. To determine whether you have a strong thumb, observe whether it reaches up to the middle of the third phalange of the index finger. This length indicates a normal thumb, longer than this is considered long, and less than this is considered short.

The man with a short index finger and a small or normal thumb will have a less severe crisis than the person with a long index finger and thumb. As we have already explained, a man with a short index finger and thumb has set his sights lower than others, has probably been fairly dependent during his life-time, and definitely does not expect many rewards out of life. Even if these two weak characteristics are combined with other strong signs (such as a good life line, good fate line, and a good Mount of Venus), middle age will not hold the same problems that await the man with a long index finger.

A long index finger and a short thumb means there is the will to achieve goals early in life because the energy and desire to work hard and achieve the goals are there. But, the energy will diminish in middle age and begin to ebb. The individual with this type of hand should begin to save for "a rainy day" early in life. He should never put things off until tomorrow, for tomorrow will find him less strong and vigorous than today.

Tracing Types of Conflicts

The conflict between a middle-aged man and his wife depends on the self-image of the man. If he has a strong index finger and thumb, he has probably been the boss in his family and is used to dominating his surroundings and making the decisions. When he faces his crisis, it will begin with a strong desire to "do something" about what he imagines to be his last few years. This type of man does not rebel; but individuals who have been imposed on, the stereotyped "hen-pecked men," the unassertive, dependent types, rebel against their wives, their jobs, or their lives. The man who has been running the show for years rarely blames others when the middle years start to bother him. On the contrary, the willing slave is the man who harbors resentment against his family and looks for sympathy and comfort from another woman. I know of many instances where a weak, dependent middle-aged man (short thumb and short index finger) has turned to a younger woman (usually neurotic and looking for a father image love object) and found himself in a worse position than the one he was trying to escape from.

An Inconclusive Conflict

An example of this is a friend of mine who fell in love with a young girl and passionately explained to me that he could not live without her, that his wife must give him a divorce and his freedom so he could marry her. Since he obviously felt so strongly about this girl, I recommended that he see a lawyer who would advise him of his legal responsibility to his wife. The lawyer naturally told him that if he divorced his wife he would be wiped out financially and lose his children. Because he was a dependent man, the thought of losing everything he had slaved for was unbearable. He was the typical middle-aged man in the vise between home, family, responsibility, and his paramour—his new love object, who made him feel potent, important, and alive again. He resolved his conflict, by keeping them both. The years go on and he maintains unhappy relationships with both these women because he lacks the courage to give either of them up.

A Conflict Solved Without Resentment

A typical example of the strong middle-aged man (long index finger and long thumb) is the man who felt the first pangs of his conflict on the golf course. He had always played in the 80's and was very proud of his prowess in this sport, perhaps more so than his success as an attorney.

His youthful "boy wonder" image was shattered the day he discovered that playing 18 holes of golf was more than pleasantly tiring but actually painful. He tried to ignore the growing feeling of apprehension about his physical condition but finally could not deny it any longer. He realized that he did not have the stamina to keep up with the young men in his golfing circle, or for that matter with his wife who was also an excellent athlete.

Gradually he began to notice fatigue in other activities as well. After many dark days of worry he consulted his doctor who told him that he was in excellent physical condition but that he was naturally getting older and that he was taxing his system too much. Being an intelligent man, he faced the fact that he would have to change his way to life to meet the demands of a new period in his life.

He turned over his pressure-ridden law practice to his junior partners, retained his interest as a consulting partner, and entered civic life. He put his experience, his years of knowledge, and his determination to work in a field that had great need of leadership. Today he is an important man in politics and while he is still no "grey-beard" he does not try to match footwork with men ten or 20 years his junior, but he leads them with his maturity. Incidentally, his marriage and his relationship with his children remained congenial because he did not blame them for his getting older. He resolved his conflict without resentment.

Incidentally, a long or "Napoleonic" index finger with a well-developed Mount of Jupiter (padding on the base of the index finger) indicates that aging for individuals with this type of finger will be especially painful because they are vain and have an inordinate love of power. These two characteristics are incompatible with aging "gracefully," since youth and beauty inevitably leave and the urge to rule remains in their place.

The Mount of Venus and the Life Line

The Mount of Venus is encircled by the life line and both indicate the energy or constitution of the individual. The Mount of Venus is the measure of the sexual vigor of the person; and, as long as the Mount of Venus is firm and muscular, you are still young no matter how many birthdays you have celebrated. If your life line is strong and the Mount of Venus is firm, your middle-age crisis will come later in your life and you probably will not suffer the impotency problems or sexual apathy and deterioration that harass so many middle-aged men. You will be virile and potent as long as you have a large, well-developed, and healthy-pink Mount of Venus. A flabby, underdeveloped Mount of Venus indicates lack of a strong sex drive. A man with a hand of this type will have trouble in middle age because a woman's sex drive usually increases during her middle years and a man with low sexual interest and capacity will have trouble satisfying what he considers her excessive demands. If a man's hand exhibits a large, strong Mount of Venus that is deep red in color, accompanied by a weak or fading fate line; shows an underdeveloped or weak head line (lack of self-control and judgment); or if there is a faulty Girdle of Venus (disturbed libido) the individual will use sex as a remedy or escape from the knowledge of failure in middle age. The tragic picture of an aging Don Juan who neglects home, family, and business for the delights of unbridled, illicit sex is well-known in literature. In real life, however, the aging Don Juan may be a man who has lost his position, failed in business, or given up the idea of success in his field.

A well-developed Mount of Venus is usually accompanied by a long life line. But, occasionally a strong Mount of Venus will have a companion life line that is weak, short, or broken. It usually is frightening for a newcomer to palmistry to discover that he has this problem life line because some so-called experts refer to this as meaning an early death. A short life line is not synonymous with a short life. It simply means that, while you will love exercise, activity, and sex (strong Mount of Venus), you must conserve your energy in middle age for you will exhaust your health and perhaps age prematurely.

The Specter of a Short Life Line

A good example of this is Mr. B. Although he is an extremely intelligent man, Mr. B was nearly scared to "death" by the specter of a short life line. Mr. B is a professional man in his early fifties. He has a strong fate line and a well-developed Mount of Venus which showed up in his love of golf, sex, and strangely enough, poker. These activities were the great loves of his life, along with his profession which required great mental activity on his part. Before his problems began he was a cynic and a religious skeptic. He began to have symptoms of fatigue and shortness of breath. He consulted a doctor and tests showed he had high blood pressure and diabetes.

His mental condition rapidly deteriorated with this news because he developed a fear of death. Somehow this cynic heard about palmistry in his search for relief from his anxiety. Instead of the relief he hoped for, he became panicky because he thought his short life line meant he would soon die. He came to me by chance and I was able to relieve his mind about this misconception. He had a long index finger, a long thumb, the strong Mount of Venus, and a short life line. I reassured him that the shortness of this line did not mean his early death but a diminishing of his energy, as evidenced by his illness.

Since his life line hugged close to his Mount of Venus, I told him he should expend major energy in mental activity of some kind other than his work. He complained to me that he had no interest in art, music, or literature and resented bitterly the fact that he would have to give up his passionate interest in golf. However, he found a solution when he decided to attend an adult Talmud class at his synagogue and soon found his skepticism and cynicism being replaced by a genuine interest in this deep, philosophical work. He soon became as much a Talmud fiend as he had formerly been a golf fiend.

To my surprise, I encountered him on the golf course one Sunday and inquired if he had given up the Talmud for the golf course once more. He laughed and explained that there was no Talmud class during the summer and he was just getting a little exercise to keep in trim. He told me that my "prescription" had been a good one for him since his blood pressure had gone back to normal and his diabetes had been controlled with one pill a day. How terrible it is for a man with high blood pressure to think that a short life line means a short life! Fortunately, Mr. B. discovered the opposite.

Indications of Difficulty by the Life Line

The life line that starts out strong but is weak or fades away at the end indicates difficulty in middle age, since it indicates a weakening of the constitution in the latter years. Conversely, a life line that is weak or badly marked in the beginning but grows stronger towards the end means that, with the acquisition of wisdom and maturity, the individual's constitution grows strong and health and vigor improve. A life line which shows an island or chain at about the middle of the hand means that the individual must be alert for physical ailments which add to the problems of adjustment to middle age. If your life line curves far out around the thumb, you must continue to be active or you will be frustrated. However, if like Mr. B., your life line hugs close to your Mount of Venus, you should pursue mental rather than physical activity. You should consider both these signs in assessing your adjustment to middle age.

The Fate Line

The consequences of the middle-age crisis depend a great deal on the fate line. This line is called the fate line because it indicates adaptability and strength of determination to overcome obstacles and reach goals. The fate line is the "stabilizer." If all the other marks and signs in your hand are good, the absence of a fate line simply means that you can probably achieve your goals with hard work but that you will have difficulty finding solutions to your problems in the middle years. A strong hand—one with many good lines—is made stronger by a good fate line (Figure 72), but a strong fate line in a strong hand does not mean that the individual will not encounter problems.

It means that he will have something extra to help him in meeting and overcoming difficulties. Sometimes a seemingly short life line may be strengthened by a strong fate line on the lower part of the hand. The life line shows the natural vitality and health of the individual but a person's determination and willpower can overcome a weak constitution. A fate line that begins strong but fades away around the head line (Figure 73) indicates that the individual will have difficulty achieving his goals after the forties or fifties, unless he has a sister line of Sun or has been extremely energetic and productive in his younger years. Again, this is a case where the adage, "Don't put off until tomorrow what you can do today," is especially applicable. A fate line that begins in the middle of the hand and extends straight up into the upper portion of the hand, usually at the base of the middle finger, is a good sign for a middle-aged man. This sign means that success will come to him after the age of 40. If he has already achieved a measure of success before 40,

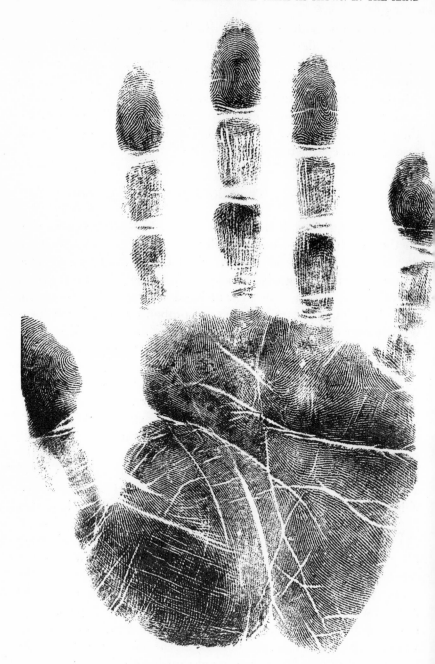

Figure 72. *A strong fate line.*

Figure 73. *The fate line on this hand ends at the head line, indicating that this man's drive and energy will end at about age 40.*

he can look forward to even greater success after this period. This does not mean that he will escape the inevitable crisis; but, his adaptability and determination will be responsible for his achievements. Truly, the old saying that life begins at 40 is true if only men and women knew how to prepare for it.

The Line of Sun or Line of Success

The fate line may be broken, weakened, or end near the heart line (traditionally, this means middle age). This is not unusual. I have observed the fate line frequently ends here (Figure 74).

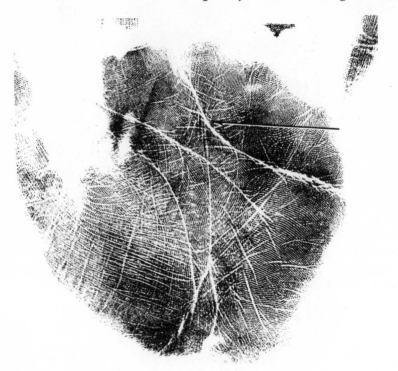

Figure 74. *The fate line on this hand ends at the heart line, indicating that his drive and energy will end at about age 50.*

It would seem that middle age ends the productive, energetic life of most people. This should not be so, but perhaps because of the popular notion that a man begins to go downhill at 40 and is ready for retirement at 65, most men are psychologically conditioned to give up their dreams and ambitions at the height of their productive years. They begin to struggle with the knowledge that they are aging and perhaps they begin to have health and love problems. These things may constitute a trauma from which they are unable to recover; or, they may expend so much energy and strength in the struggle that they have nothing left for achievement. I believe this is the reason I so seldom see a fate line that does not end in the middle of the palm (i.e., middle years).

Some individuals, however, have a sister line to the fate line. This line, known as the Sun line or line of success, begins at the heart line under the ring finger in most individuals (Figure 75). In some instances, it begins in the middle of the palm and runs up to the base of the ring finger (Figure 76).

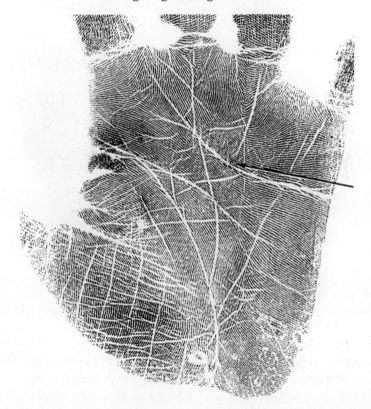

Figure 75. *The line of Sun in this hand starts at the heart line.*

The higher in the hand this line begins, the later success will be achieved. It acts as a complement to the fate line. If for some reason the fate line ends at middle age, the line of Sun takes over and gives the necessary strength to win over adversity. When this line is seen in a hand, you know that individual will win success after 40 and directly as a result of the efforts that he expends after this period in life. It should be a tremendously encouraging sign for a middle-aged man to find this line in his

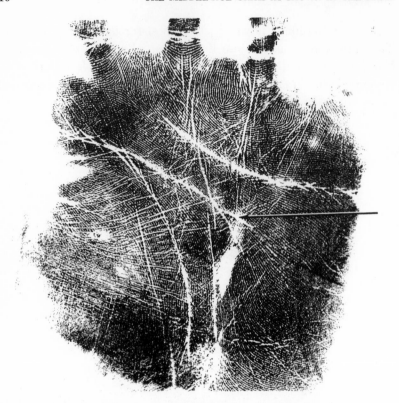

Figure 76. *The line of Sun in this hand starts in the middle of the palm.*

hand because when everything looks black and there seems to be no end in sight for his suffering, he can be reassured that conditions will soon improve for him. A fate line that reaches to the base of the middle finger and a Sun line that also reaches to the ring finger indicates that middle age will not signal the end of the career of a person's dreams but the beginning of a bigger success.

If a man has no fate line and no success line and an undeveloped, short thumb, he must depend on his wife to supply the strength that he lacks. Hopefully, he will find that his wife has a strong hand that counterbalances his weaknesses. If, however, her hand is weak and she acts as a drag on him in his conflict, he probably will seek out someone who can supply him with extra impetus and perhaps even leave his wife.

The hand cannot reveal the man's relationship with women. It cannot tell about his relationship with his mother or with his wife, but these two factors are highly important and are closely related to the problems of middle age. At middle age, a man who is emotionally attached to his mother may have two very real problems. His mother is becoming senile or may die at this time. His wife may be experiencing her menopause and is extremely hard to get along with. For many men, a wife is a mother substitute to whom he has been accustomed to turn for help and reassurance. When his real mother dies or becomes lost to him through the aging process, he tends to turn more to his wife and it is at this precise point that she fails to "come through" for him. She is going through a crisis herself and fails to realize that her husband is facing one, a critical one, himself.

Almost always a middle-aged man turns to some woman for comfort in the middle-age crisis. Many middle-aged women seem to find it improbable that a very young woman could be a proper "mother substitute" for a middle-aged man. The middle-aged wife fails to realize that a kind, sympathetic attitude on the part of any woman is an irresistible attraction to a troubled man. Since her husband will turn to her first, a wise woman will recognize her strengths and weaknesses from her hand and use them to help her husband through this period. The husband, himself, should make use of this knowledge to know both his own and his wife's strengths and weaknesses and gain knowledge about the areas in their lives which need work and effort.

Questions the Wife Should Ask Herself

The question every wife should ask herself is whether or not she is prepared to lose her husband, as much as she may resent him. Is she prepared to become a divorcee, a widow, or a betrayed woman? She could very easily become any of these by refusing to face facts or by continuing to offer her husband nothing but recriminations and abuse.

She could become a widow by continuing to drive her husband to provide more and more material benefits past his endurance to achieve.

A common, pathetic sight is the coveys of middle-aged widows who adorn resorts and luxury hotels and apartments hungrily looking for an eligible husband to take the place of the husband they may have driven to death. Of course, their search is futile because they are looking for a rich man who will match their wealth, offer security, and yet love them for themselves. This combination is impossible for them to find. They do not have the physical or mental capabilities to attract a man of that caliber. If they find a man willing to put up with them, it is usually someone who is interested in getting as much of their wealth as possible before abandoning them for the next "victim."

A middle-aged woman can also become the betrayed woman, and this is common. Even though a man may continue to live with her out of loyalty for past sacrifices, because of business or family, or because he lacks the courage to leave her, he must find comfort in the arms of a woman somewhere. His wife is then betrayed because she refuses to face facts and see that his crisis is more serious than hers and should take precedence over hers.

If a man has a short thumb, he needs lots of reassurance. Surely, any wife who values her husband can provide this. If a man has a fading fate line, his wife should not drive him because he has done what he can for her. If he has a short life line, she must not drive him because she will surely drive him to his grave. This last statement is indeed strong, but my experience leads me to believe that those with a short life line must conserve their energy in middle age or they will succumb to the pressure.

Two case histories illustrate my point concerning the therapeutic knowledge or value of hand analysis and the important role of the wife in the middle-age crisis.

An Advertising Executive's Experience

An advertising executive in his forties was conforming to the pattern so closely associated with others in his trade. He worked hard, bowled, and drank somewhat more than the average fellow. He was married and had two children. He was 30 pounds overweight and often felt tired and tense. He did not consult a doctor because he did not feel he needed medical help.

One day, on his way to the bank, he was invited to take a free chest x-ray in a mobile truck. His first impulse was to refuse but, since he had the time, he allowed them to take an x-ray. He soon received a letter advising him, although he did not have tuberculosis, that he should consult his doctor regarding his enlarged heart. Subsequently, his doctor confirmed that he had a large heart.

Because the patient did not experience shortness of breath or swelling of his ankles, the doctor did not prescribe medicine but gave him a list of rules that he found crushing and demoralizing. The doctor ordered him to stop drinking and smoking, to reduce 30 pounds, and to work less. The patient found it next to impossible to follow his orders and became more tense than ever. He worried himself to the point that his sex drive disappeared and with it all his wife nagged, accused him of infidelity, and drove him to distraction with petty bickering.

He consulted me in a state of acute anxiety, asking for a remedy for his impotency. I noticed his rather large hands and asked him for the x-ray that had caused all his anxiety. On examining the x-ray, I found that his heart was the same size as his clenched fist—a sign that the heart size was normal for him. After giving him other tests, I determined that his heart function was normal. I advised him to stop dieting, to smoke moderately, to limit his drinking to a more reasonable amount, and most importantly, I advised him to stop worrying about his sexual performance. I could tell by his Mount of Venus that he would be potent into old age and told him so. Some years later I met this gentleman on the street, accompanied by a stunning female companion. He informed me that my advice had restored his hope and confidence in himself. He smiled broadly when he bragged that he had licked his potency problem; his companion confirmed this point most enthusiastically. I asked him what had happened to his wife, and growing serious he replied that unfortunately his wife had proved to him conclusively during his crisis that she was not his friend. Her terrible behavior toward him in this period led to divorce, but he said unequivocally that he had never regretted his decision. He had found love and understanding in another woman, who had "befriended" him in his trouble.

The other example involves fate in the life of one man. This man was successful, had good relations with his wife, and held a good job which gave him much satisfaction. Fate stepped into this happy picture and delivered a low blow. This man had an accident which put him out of work for many months. He lost his job and his wife cracked under the strain and left him for another man. Deprived of everything, he began to drink heavily after his convalescence. He lost all hope of ever becoming a normal human being again. I met him on a Chicago street that is known as the last step down for many disillusioned men. I read his palm and saw that he had a broken fate line which could have foretold his difficulty. I did not mention this fact, however, but I told him that he had an excellent heart line and life line. He had a wonderful line of Sun which meant his success would begin after 40. He considered palmistry nonsense and could not accept my prophecy. Time proved me right. He met another, stronger woman who gave him the courage to begin again. They now own three very successful businesses in town and this man made a special effort to tell me that, while he had been a skeptic, the hope and faith I had given him had benefited him in finding his new life.

IV

ANALYSIS OF
PALM PRINTS

19

Analysis of Characteristics of Different Palm Prints

Following are some significant palm prints analyzed for your guidance in building a considered judgment of palmar indications. Each illustration has a brief description as to important conclusions. (See next page.)

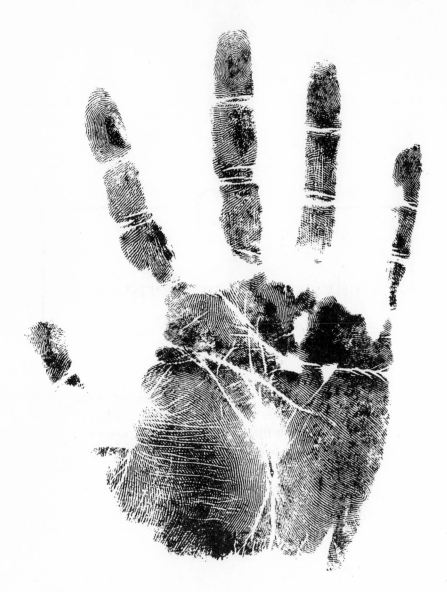

Figure I-a. *The imprint of a contented man. The initial M is well delineated and developed. The fingers are long and straight. No accessory lines, indicating subject is calm in great emergencies. The long fate line signifies that he can well adjust to every life situation, accepting whatever comes philosophically. As he concluded, "I enjoy all the good things in life and don't let the unpleasant things faze me."*

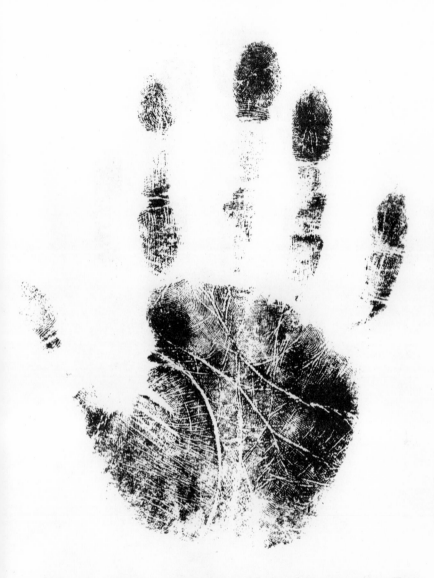

Figure I-b. *This is a very good female hand. In contrast to Figure I-a the main crease lines are not so deep and strong and there are more accessory lines, indicating greater sensitivity. Also the head line and the life line are widely separated (whereas those of Figure I-a are closer together), signifying a typical female trait—impulsiveness and unpredictability. Note the unusually beautiful, long life line.*

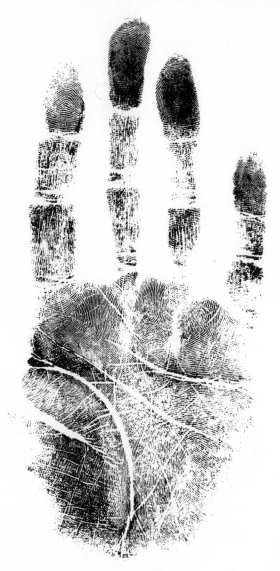

Figure II-a. *The subject of this print has a perfect life line and an especially good head line, indicating that he has a healthy mind and a healthy body, the two great components of happiness. Nevertheless he is unhappy because he feels "lonely and unlucky in love." The short and faulty heart line indicates that he is incapable of giving or accepting love. The short little finger shows lack of ability to communicate. The weak fate line tells us he cannot adjust to disappointments in love.*

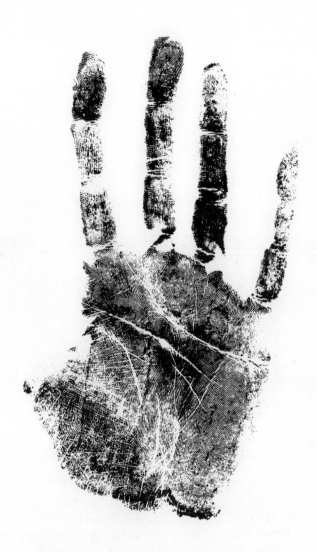

Figure II-b. *In contrast, the palm of this subject indicates a happy and healthy individual, despite the fact that she has one of the poorest life lines I ever examined and a bad fate line. But she has a long and good head line, and an especially long and beautiful heart line. We can truly say of the owner of this palm, "Love conquers all"—especially since her well-developed little finger shows the faculty of communication.*

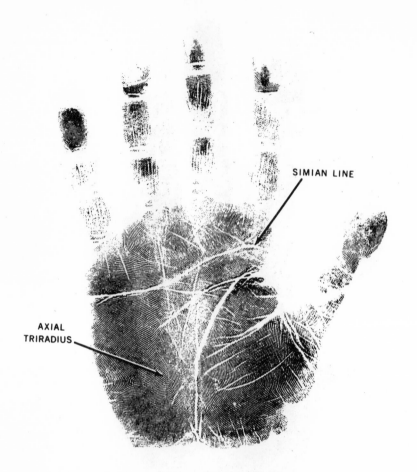

SIMIAN LINE

AXIAL
TRIRADIUS

Figure III. *This is a paradoxical masculine hand. Although perfectly shaped, its palm print reveals some atavistic features, such as a short head line, a simian line, and a highly placed axial triradius, the normal location of which is the bottom of the palm.*

The palm print aberration indicates that something injurious happened to the mother during the period of pregnancy. The well-developed physiognomy of the hand, however, reveals, as the subject confirmed, that his life situation was satisfactory during the growth period. The well-developed thumb and index finger indicate a strong ego structure. The little finger tells us, by its length, of his ability to communicate, besides indicating executive ability. We would call this a well-compensated hand.

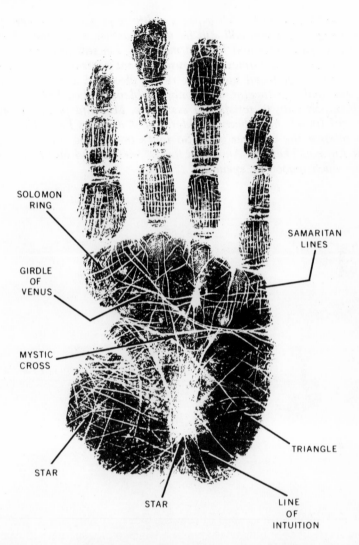

SOLOMON
RING

SAMARITAN
LINES

GIRDLE
OF
VENUS

MYSTIC
CROSS

TRIANGLE

STAR

STAR

LINE
OF
INTUITION

Figure IV. *This palm has almost every sign and line in the book of palmistry—the Solomon ring, the Samaritan line, the mystic cross, the line of intuition, the Venus Girdle, and a well-delineated initial M. It also contains various symbols such as the square, the triangle, and stars. It is interesting to note that the subject's character coincides with the interpretation of the palmist. He appears to be what his hand says he is.*

When I analyzed his hand he was 61 years old, and at that time I told him that all these signs indicated he had a powerful vitality, *activity, and an interest in all aspects of life. I predicted, "When you are an octogenarian you will still be young, active, and virile." I met this man 16 years later and he told me, "Yes, I'm still practicing law, but not so much as formerly because I want to travel extensively. I still enjoy my golf and horseback riding also, and attend concerts, the opera, and the theater. The only problem is that I don't have enough opportunity to satisfy my sex drive. My wife passed away— all my girl friends have become elderly, and it seems I'm getting too old to interest the younger ones. So that's one of the reasons I like to visit Europe. There an American tourist isn't judged by his age but by how much money he spends."*

Figure V. *The keynote of this print is a perfect fate line and a good heart line, which compensate for the subject's inferiority complex, tendency to worry, and extreme sensitivity. Head and life lines are joined in the beginning, and there is a Venus Girdle. The fate line is crossed by several lines, which indicate obstacles in the pathway of his destiny. It matters not whether this assumption is true, for the strong fate line and heart line indicate that he can say, "All's well that ends well."*

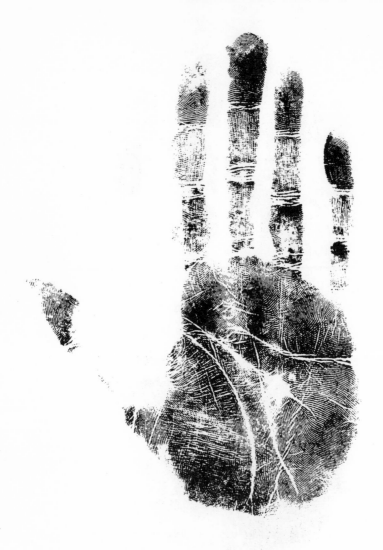

Figure VI. *This palm print has the signs of the classic example of the emancipated American female. She has a powerful head line (strong vitality) long index finger (egoism, aggressiveness, and domination), a well-developed little finger (executive ability), and a strong thumb (willpower). Her strong fate line emphasizes the qualities which enable her to accomplish anything a man can do—or more. Nevertheless she is representative of the modern American syndrome—she has everything but love. She has a very poor and short heart line.*

Figure VII. *This is the print of a pathetic male who is eternally searching for and failing to find affection and love. He has two heart lines, signifying that to him love and affection are indispensable and the most important drive. But both are short and faulty, indicating he is not capable of accepting and receiving love. And, having no fate line, he is not able to fulfill his desires. If a person has one heart line, short and faulty, he may search for love, but not finding it immediately, will give up the search, for love to him is animalistic.*

Figure VIII. *The outstanding feature of this palm print is that all the fingers have a whorl pattern and the fate line is unusually long and strong. This is the sign of an independent and strong personality. According to Y. Miyamoto, noted Japanese fingerprint expert, five whorls signify a self-respecting and outspoken individual who has a stern and clear-cut attitude toward political and social issues. He calls it a "lordly type" or "a lone tree in the middle of a plain." Such a subject is destined to create his own fortune and remain healthy into old age without being dependent on his children or charity. In other words, he can master his own destiny. This is exactly what the second feature, the long, straight fate line indicates.*

Figure IX. *In contrast to the strong fate line of Figure VIII, this print has no fate line at all. It is a primitive and elementary hand, with short thumb, thenar eminence (Mount of Venus) well-developed, and life line long and deep. The hand is relatively large, muscular, and has a coarse skin. The palm has few lines, characterizing lack of sensitivity. These individuals don't expect too much of life so long as they have food, sex, and shelter.*

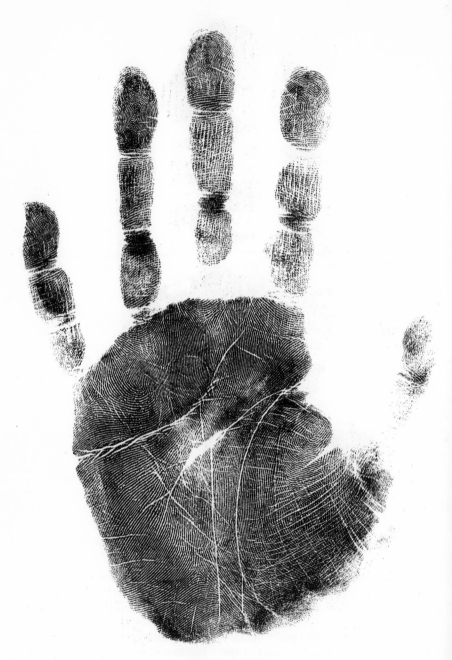

Figure X. *Rose.*

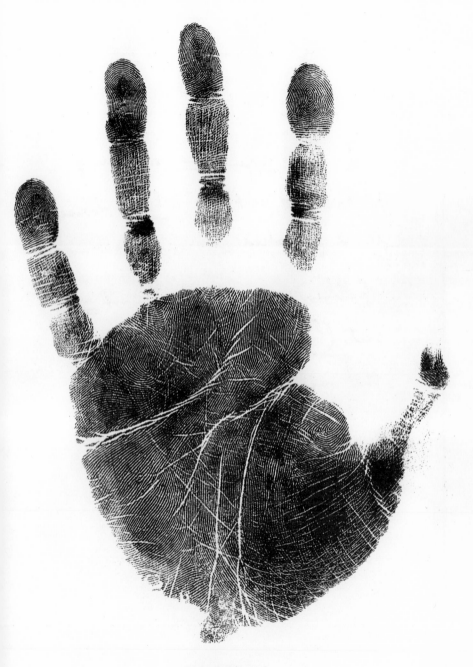

Figure XI. *Lily.*

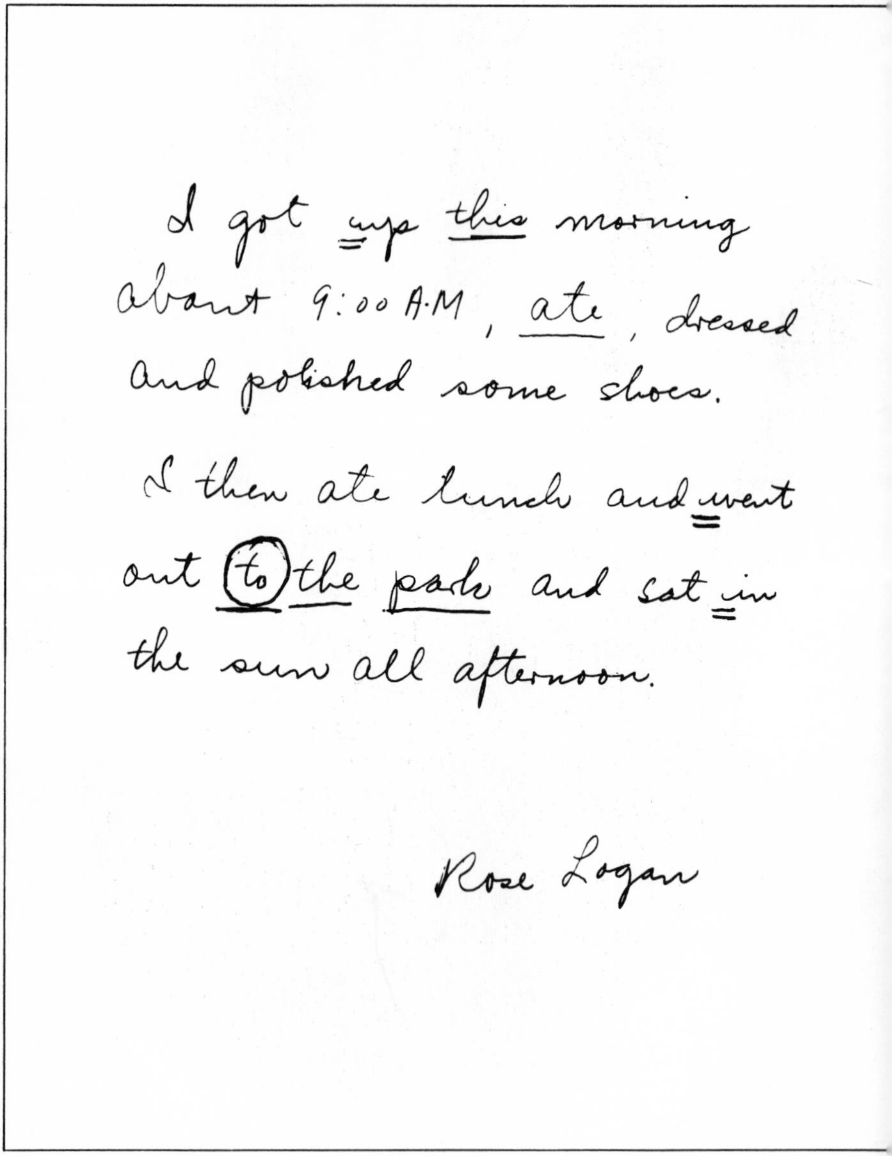

I got up this morning about 9:00 A.M , ate , dressed and polished some shoes.

I then ate lunch and went out to the park and sat in the sun all afternoon.

Rose Logan

Figure X-a.

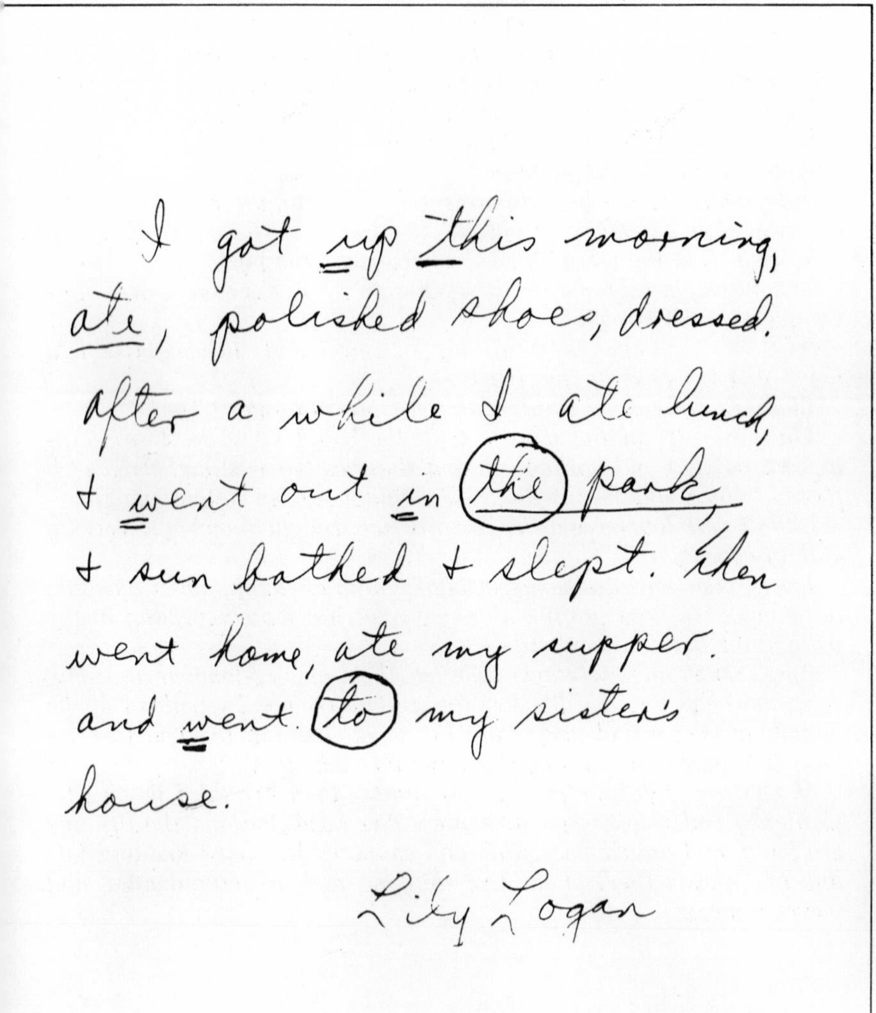

I got up this morning,
ate, polished shoes, dressed.
After a while I ate lunch,
& went out in (the) park,
& sun bathed & slept. Then
went home, ate my supper.
and went (to) my sister's
house.

Lily Logan

Figure XI-a.

Figure X and XI. *These are the palm prints of identical twin females, Rose and Lily. The prints look alike. The women are the same size, have exactly the same body build, weigh the same, and their handwriting is remarkably similar. The palm prints, especially the axial triradii and the directions of the crease lines, are almost identical. Nevertheless, with respect to the two most important personality traits, these females are entirely dissimilar. Rose, Figure X, is dominating, calm, and has a positive attitude toward life, while Lily is very dependent, cautious, and insecure.*

Independence, and in certain respects maturity, are revealed by the absence of a beginning stroke, as illustrated in Rose's handwriting (Figure X-a) in the words "these," "two," and "the park."

In contrast, in Lily's handwriting (Figure XI-a), the same words have complete initial strokes.

In Rose's writing, the words "up," "went," and "in" begin with a hook, showing tenacity and persistence.

Lily writes the same words with the childish initial stroke.

The letter "t" in the words "to," "the," and "this" in Rose's writing are pointed and not looped, and the crossbar is straight and well placed, which signifies dignity, self-confidence, and determination.

Lily's t's are looped and the bars are not straight showing sensitivity and insecurity.

These character traits, especially the domination, determination, self-confidence, and positive thinking ones are more revealing in the palm print than in handwriting.

Rose's index finger is larger than her third finger (dominance, strong ego); her head line and life line are well marked and separated at the beginning (self-confidence). Both the head line and the fate line are long and unbroken (positive thinking, determination).

In contrast, Lily's index finger is shorter than her third finger (dependency and weaker ego structure). The head line and the life line are faulty and united (insecurity and caution). Her head line and fate line are broken (lack of positive thinking and of determination and perseverance).

Index

235

Scheimann

A doctor's guide to better health through palmistry

DATE DUE		
FEB 2 9 1973		
SEP 2 6 1973		
OCT 1 0 1973		
OCT 3 1 1973		
JAN 2 7 1974		
MAY 1 0 1974		
APR 1 8 1975		
MAY 2 6 1975		
JUN 9 '75		
FEB 7 1977		
NOV 11 81		
APR 1 3 1998		
GAYLORD		PRINTED IN U.S.A.